THE AUSTRALIAN
Women's Weekly

The PIE MAKER

VOLUME 2

The PIE MAKER

VOLUME 2

CONTENTS

MORE PIES

When we launched our first book, *The Pie Maker* we were confident in the recipes, a labour of love made possible by cook Bree Hutchinson, who honed them during the recipe-testing, styling and photography stages. It takes a team to make a book, so behind it all, there was our experienced editor, Stephanie Kistner and creative director Hannah Blackmore, who also donned hats as taste testers and sounding boards for new ideas. Nevertheless, none of us anticipated its runaway success, or that pie making machines would be embraced so whole-heartedly by the wider community, spawning multiple Facebook groups and pages, where the pie-obsessed share their experiences and ideas, and our book. Of which, we are most grateful! Far from having exhausted the possibilities of the machine, for Vol 2 we set out with a larger team to showcase that 'the pie's the limit'. There are pies, sweet and savoury treats, snacks, celebration cakes, breakfast ideas and the ulitmate hack – dinner and dessert for one! Again, we hope you enjoy making these recipes as much as we did creating them.

SIZE MATTERS Most brands of pie makers are designed to make four individual pies and are similar to operate. The main difference between brands lies in the size of the pies they make. One of the most popular machines makes ⅓-cup (80ml) pies, however there are also machines for larger ¾-cup (180ml) pies, 2-hole (100ml) pies and even those that produce a single 2½-cup (625ml) family-sized pie. The majority of the recipes in this book are for a 4-hole (⅓-cup/80ml) pie maker, but there are several recipes designed for a 4-hole (¾-cup/180ml) and a 2-hole (100ml) pie maker, plus a sprinkling of sweet and savoury options for family-sized pies. Regardless of the machine you have, once you know the capacity of each hole, you can adapt the amount of filling you need for your particular machine. Alternatively, simply aim to always leave a 2mm (1/12in) gap between the top of the filling and the rim of the pastry before cooking a tart, or covering with pastry for a pie, unless otherwise specified in a recipe. Before you start making any recipes in this book, determine the capacity of the individual holes of your pie maker. To do this, fill a small measuring cup with water and fill a pie hole to the brim. As a guide, these are the hole capacities for the four most common machines:

4-hole (⅓-cup/80ml) each hole will hold approximately ¼ cup filling.

4-hole (¾-cup/180ml) each hole will hold approximately ⅔ cup filling.

2-hole (100ml) each hole will hold approximately ⅓ cup filling.

family-sized single pie holds approximately 2⅓ cups filling.

TO BE PIE-READY, CUT OUT ROUNDS OF PASTRY AHEAD OF TIME AND STORE IN THE FREEZER.

Take care not to over fill your pies or they will make a mess. You can always check one pie before filling them all. It is also important to read your pie makers' instruction manual for further specific guidance around use.

UTENSILS Your pie maker has a non-stick coating, which is best preserved by using non-stick cooking utensils. Most pie makers come equipped with a cutter designed to cut out both the bottom and top rounds of pastry to fit the brand of pie maker. However, each of our recipes also notes the size of the pastry rounds required.

CLEANING When making multiple batches of pies, wipe the pie holes clean with a damp piece of paper towel and avoid the use of abrasive cleaning agents.

PASTRY The best combination for most pies (or for tart bases) is a shortcrust base for crispness and then either a puff pastry or shortcrust top. For speed, pastry rounds can be cut to size and stored in the freezer so you have them on hand.

PREPPING Meat pie fillings can all be made ahead and refrigerated. They also freeze well. To reheat frozen pies, place ⅓-cup (80ml) pies in the pie maker for 14 minutes and ¾-cup (180ml) pies for 12 minutes. (Note that the pastry will continue to brown.) Alternatively, reheat in a 180°C/350°F oven for 15 minutes.

HOLDING THE MACHINE LID AJAR Use a heatproof object, such as a wooden spoon or a narrow roll of paper towel as a wedge at the front of the machine to prevent the lid from squashing the contents. We suggest an object that will prop the lid ajar by 2cm (¾in).

HOMEMADE PASTRY

Roll out each portion of pastry between two floured sheets of baking paper (dust with the same type of flour as used in the pastry recipe) until approximately 24cm x 25cm (9½in x 10in) – the equivalent size of a bought pastry sheet. Continue as directed in the recipe. You will need to adjust the cooking time slightly depending on the pastry you are using. Shortcrust pastry and cream cheese pastry may also be frozen for up to 2 months, wrapped in an airtight container. Thaw in the fridge overnight before using.

SHORTCRUST PASTRY

PREP 15 MINUTES MAKES 2 SHEETS

1¾ cups (260g) plain (all-purpose) flour • 150g (4½oz) cold butter, chopped coarsely • 1 egg yolk • 2 teaspoons lemon juice • 1 tablespoon iced water

Process flour and butter until it resembles crumbs. Add egg yolk, lemon juice and iced water; pulse until ingredients just cling together. Knead gently on a floured surface until smooth. Divide dough in 2. Wrap separately; refrigerate 30 minutes until ready to use. See above for rolling instructions. Makes 425g/13½oz.

CREAM CHEESE PASTRY

PREP 15 MINUTES MAKES 5 SHEETS

300g (9½oz) cold butter, chopped • 250g (8oz) cream cheese, softened, chopped • 3⅓ cups (500g) plain (all-purpose) flour • ½ cup (110g) caster (superfine) sugar • ½ cup (120g) sour cream

Process butter, cream cheese, flour and sugar until mixture starts to clump. (For a savoury pastry omit the sugar.) Add sour cream; process until ingredients just come together. Form doung into a ball. Divide dough into 5. Wrap separately; refrigerate 30 minutes or until ready to use. See above for rolling instructions. Makes 1.2kg/2½lb.

KETO PASTRY

PREP 15 MINUTES MAKES 2½ SHEETS

3 cups (360g) almond meal • 3 eggs, beaten lightly • ½ teaspoon fine salt • ½ cup (60g) tapioca flour, approximately, plus extra for dusting

Stir all ingredients in a large bowl until a soft, sticky dough forms. Turn onto a bench sprinkled with tapioca flour; form dough into a ball. Add extra tapioca flour if dough is too sticky. Divide dough into 2½. Wrap; stand at room temperature until ready to use. See above for rolling instructions. Makes 570g/1¼lb.

GLUTEN-FREE PASTRY

PREP TIME 15 MINUTES MAKES 3 SHEETS

375g (12oz) packet gluten-free pastry mix • 125g (4oz) cold butter, chopped • ⅔ cup (160ml) water • 2 tablespoons gluten-free tamari • 2 tablespoons olive oil • gluten-free plain (all-purpose) flour, for dusting

Process pastry mix and butter until mixture resembles coarse breadcrumbs. Add enough of the combined water, tamari and oil until mixture comes together. Lightly knead on a surface dusted with a little gluten-free flour into a ball. Divide dough into 3. See above for rolling instructions. Makes 625g/1¼lb.

tip Pastry is best used straightaway.

SAVOURY PIES

MEATBALL SUB PIES

PREP + COOK TIME
30 MINUTES

MAKES 8

500g (1lb) pork and fennel sausages

1 tablespoon olive oil

1 cup (260g) bottled arrabbiata pasta sauce

8 x 8cm (3¼in) round dinner rolls (60g each)

60g (2oz) baby rocket (arugula) leaves

1 cup (80g) coarsely grated parmesan

1 Slit sausages at the top with a sharp knife; squeeze out sausage meat from casings. Roll into 24 balls (this is about 3 teaspoons each). Heat oil in a large frying pan over medium heat; cook meatballs, for 4 minutes, turning, until almost cooked through. Add pasta sauce; cook, stirring, for 3 minutes or until thickened slightly. Cool.

2 Grease and preheat a 2-hole (100ml) pie maker.

3 Using a serrated knife, cut tops off the rolls. Remove the centre of the roll, leaving a 5mm (¼in) shell.

4 Place four hollowed rolls in prepared holes; place a small handfull of rocket leaves (5g) in each. Fill with three meatballs and some sauce then top each with 1 tablespoon of the parmesan. Cover with the bread tops. Close lid; cook for 5 minutes or until bread is well browned and filling heated through. Repeat with remaining hollowed rolls, rocket, meatballs, parmesan and bread tops.

5 Serve pies with remaining rocket and remaining parmesan.

COOK'S NOTE

To make these in a smaller pie maker, see page 7 for information on how much filling they hold, then adjust accordingly. You will need smaller bread rolls.

COOK'S NOTE
Cooked spanakopita can be frozen for up to 2 months. Thaw in fridge overnight. Reheat in pie maker for 8 minutes.

SPANAKOPITA SPIRAL

PREP + COOK TIME
35 MINUTES

SERVES 4

We used a family-size pie maker for this recipe.

6 sheets fillo pastry, thawed if frozen

extra virgin olive oil spray

2 teaspoons fennel seeds

lemon wedges, to serve

SPINACH FILLING

300g (9½oz) frozen spinach, thawed

3 green onions (scallions), chopped finely

150g (4½oz) fetta, crumbled

⅓ cup (80g) firm ricotta, crumbled

¼ cup finely chopped dill

2 tablespoons finely chopped mint

1 To make spinach filling, squeeze excess moisture from spinach, then finely chop. Combine spinach with remaining filling ingredients in a medium bowl. (Makes 2 cups.)

2 Layer 3 sheets of fillo, spraying each sheet with oil. Repeat with remaining sheets and more oil spray to make two fillo stacks. Cut each stack in half lengthways.

3 Lightly grease and preheat a family-size (2½-cup/625ml) pie maker. Using the smaller pastry cutter provided, trace a 23cm (9¼in) round on a sheet of baking paper; cut out the round.

4 Working quickly, divide filling into three portions. Place one portion of filling lengthways in a thin line, along the edge of one pastry rectangle; roll pastry over to cover filling. Starting at the centre of the baking paper round, carefully form the pastry roll, seam-side down, into a spiral. Repeat with two more pastry rectangles and remaining filling portions, joining each roll to the end of the last one and coiling them around to form a spiral pie. You will have one pastry rectangle left; keep for another use (see page 157.)

5 Carefully lift spiral on paper into pie maker; spray generously with oil and scatter with seeds. Close lid; cook for 25 minutes, spraying again with oil halfway through cooking, or until pastry is golden. Remove spanakopita; transfer to a wire rack to cool.

6 Serve spanakopita straightaway with lemon wedges.

BROCCOLI CHEESE PIES

PREP + COOK TIME
40 MINUTES

MAKES 8

1 cup (70g) fresh coarse breadcrumbs (see page 158)

2 teaspoons finely chopped rosemary

2 cloves garlic, crushed

250g (8oz) very small broccoli florets, cooked

2 sheets frozen puff pastry, thawed

cooking oil spray

CHEESE SAUCE

1½ tablespoons butter, softened

2 cloves garlic, crushed

1½ tablespoons plain flour (all-purpose flour)

1⅓ cups (330ml) milk

1½ teaspoons dijon mustard

½ teaspoon chilli flakes

⅛ teaspoon ground nutmeg

¼ cup (30g) coarsely grated cheddar

2 tablespoons finely grated parmesan

1 Combine breadcrumbs, rosemary and garlic in a small bowl.

2 To make cheese sauce, heat butter and garlic in a small saucepan over medium heat, add flour; cook until mixture bubbles and thickens. Gradually add milk, whisking until sauce boils and thickens. Remove from heat; stir in remaining ingredients until cheeses melt. Season to taste. (Makes 2 cups.)

3 Add broccoli to cheese sauce; stir to combine.

4 Lightly grease and preheat a 4-hole (⅓-cup/80ml) pie maker.

5 Using pastry cutter provided, cut eight large rounds (11cm/4½in) from puff pastry. Line prepared holes with pastry rounds, pressing into base and side. Refrigerate remaining pastry rounds until required.

6 Spoon ¼ cup broccoli sauce into each pie case, then top with 1 tablespoon breadcrumb mixture; spray pies with oil. Close lid; cook for 13 minutes or until breadcrumbs are golden brown. Remove pies; transfer to a wire rack. Repeat with remaining pastry rounds, broccoli sauce and breadcrumb mixture.

COOK'S NOTE

Broccoli cheese pies can be frozen in an airtight container for up to 2 months. Thaw in fridge overnight. Reheat in the pie maker for 8 minutes.

COOK'S NOTE

To make these in a smaller pie maker, see page 7 for information on how much filling they hold, then adjust accordingly.

FISH & CHIP PIES

PREP + COOK TIME
45 MINUTES

MAKES 6

30g (1oz) butter

2 tablespoons plain flour (all-purpose flour)

1 cup (250ml) fish stock

½ cup (55g) grated 3 cheese mix

400g (12½oz) boneless, skinless salmon, cut into 2cm (¾in) pieces

1 tablespoon chopped chives

2 teaspoons finely grated lemon rind

2 tablespoons capers, chopped

1½ sheets frozen shortcrust pastry, thawed

240g (7½oz) frozen shoestring fries, thawed

cooking oil spray

lemon wedges and cooked extra shoestring fries, to serve

1 Melt butter in a medium saucepan over medium heat. Add flour; cook, stirring for 1 minute. Remove from heat and gradually stir in stock. Return to heat; cook, whisking, for 3 minutes or until mixture boils and thickens. Whisk in the cheese mix. Add fish; cook, stirring occasionally, for 3 minutes or until just cooked through. Stir in chives, lemon rind and capers; season. Cool. (Makes 2 cups.)

2 Lightly grease and preheat a 2-hole (100ml) pie maker.

3 Using pastry cutter provided, cut six large rounds (12cm/4¾in) from shortcrust pastry. Line prepared holes with pastry rounds, pressing into base and side. Refrigerate remaining rounds until required.

4 Spoon ⅓ cup fish mixture into each pastry case. Place fries over the filling, arranging them, side-by-side in one direction (don't worry if they extend slightly beyond the round). Spray fries with oil, close lid; cook pies for 8 minutes or until golden. Remove pies; transfer to a wire rack. Repeat in batches with remaining pastry rounds, fish mixture, fries and more oil spray.

5 Serve pies immediately with lemon wedges and extra fries.

BEAN & CORN TACO PIES

PREP + COOK TIME
50 MINUTES

MAKES 6

1 tablespoon butter

2 corn cobs (900g), trimmed, kernels cut off

1 fresh jalapeño chilli, chopped finely

6 x 12cm (4¾in) white corn mini tortillas

½ cup (60g) grated cheddar

1 cup (80g) shredded cos lettuce

½ cup (120g) guacamole

9 grape tomatoes (45g), quartered

½ cup (100g) sour cream

coriander (cilantro) leaves and lime wedges, to serve

TACO FILLING

1 tablespoon olive oil

1 small clove garlic, crushed

1 tablespoon finely chopped coriander stalks

1 teaspoon sweet paprika

1 teaspoon ground coriander

400g (12½oz) can black beans, drained, rinsed

¾ cup (170g) enchilada sauce

1 Heat butter in a large frying pan over medium heat; cook corn kernels and jalapeño, stirring, for 10 minutes or until corn is tender. Remove from pan; set aside.

2 To make taco filling, heat oil in same frying pan over medium heat; cook garlic and coriander stalks, stirring, for 2 minutes. Add spices and beans; cook, stirring, for 2 minutes or until beans are heated through. Add sauce; cook, stirring occasionally, for 5 minutes or until sauce thickens. Season to taste. Cool. (Makes 1 cup.) Add half the corn mixture to the beans; reserve remaining to serve.

3 Lightly grease and preheat a 4-hole (⅓-cup/80ml) pie maker. Wrap tortillas in paper towel; heat in the microwave on HIGH (100%) for 40 seconds. Keep warm in a clean tea towel. (Heating the tortillas will make them more pliable, preventing them from tearing.) Line prepared holes with four tortillas, press into base and side.

4 Spoon 2 heaped tablespoons taco filling and 1 tablespoon cheddar into each tortilla case. Close lid; cook for 6 minutes or until cheese melts. Remove taco pies; transfer to a wire rack. Repeat with remaining tortillas, taco filling and cheddar.

5 Top pies with lettuce, guacamole, reserved corn mixture, tomatoes, sour cream and coriander leaves; serve with lime wedges.

COOK'S NOTE

If you are using frozen fillo pastry, thaw the pastry in the fridge the night before.

POTATO & PEA SAMOSA PIES

PREP + COOK TIME
50 MINUTES

MAKES 8

2 sheets fillo pastry
cooking oil spray
1 teaspoon caraway seeds
mango chutney and yoghurt, to serve

POTATO FILLING
20g (¾oz) butter
2 teaspoons olive oil
½ medium onion (100g), sliced thinly
1 clove garlic, crushed
2 teaspoons grated ginger
½ long green chilli, sliced thinly
¼ teaspoon garam masala
½ teaspoon ground cumin
150g (5½oz) potato, boiled, mashed coarsely
¼ cup (30g) frozen peas, thawed

1 To make potato filling, heat butter and oil in a medium frying pan over medium heat; cook onion, garlic, ginger and chilli, stirring, for 5 minutes or until softened. Add spices; cook, stirring, for 5 minutes. Season. Combine onion mixture, potato and peas in a medium bowl. (Makes 1 cup).

2 Spray 1 sheet fillo pastry with oil; cut crossways into four rectangles. On each rectangle, place 1 heaped tablespoon of potato filling 2cm (¾in) up from the bottom of a short side and 2cm (¾in) in on each side. Fold bottom edge over to enclose filling, then fold in the sides; continue folding over to form a parcel. Repeat with remaining fillo sheet and filling to make eight in total.

3 Lightly grease and preheat a 4-hole (¾-cup/180ml) pie maker.

4 Place four parcels in prepared holes, spray tops with oil then sprinkle with half the caraway seeds. Close lid; cook for 10 minutes each side or until pastry is golden. Remove samosas; transfer to a wire rack. Repeat with remaining parcels, oil spray and caraway seeds.

5 Serve samosa pies with mango chutney and yoghurt.

LAMB PITTA PIES WITH HUMMUS

PREP + COOK TIME
20 MINUTES

MAKES 8

8 small pitta breads
cooking oil spray
½ cup (130g) hummus
½ cup (100g) fetta, crumbled
chopped flat-leaf parsley and lemon wedges, to serve

LAMB FILLING
500g (1lb) lamb sausages
1 tablespoon olive oil
1 clove garlic, crushed
¼ cup (45g) grilled marinated eggplant, chopped
¼ cup (60g) roasted red capsicum (bell pepper), chopped
1 teaspoon finely grated lemon rind
¼ cup chopped flat-leaf parsley
2 tablespoons chopped mint

1 To make lamb filling, slit the sausages along the top with a sharp knife; squeeze out sausage meat from casings. Heat oil in a large frying pan. Cook sausage meat and garlic, stirring with a wooden spoon to break up lumps, for 5 minutes or until browned. Stir in eggplant, capsicum, lemon rind and herbs; cook, stirring, for a further 5 minutes. Season. Cool. (Makes 2 cups.)

2 Lightly grease and preheat a 4-hole (⅓-cup/80ml) pie maker.

3 Using pastry cutter provided, cut eight large rounds (11cm/4½in) from pitta breads. Microwave four pitta rounds on LOW (50%) for 30 seconds to soften. Immediately line prepared holes with softened pitta rounds.

4 Spoon a heaped ¼ cup lamb filling into each pitta case. Spray tops with oil. Close lid; cook for 5 minutes or until pitta is crisp. Remove pies; transfer to a wire rack. Microwave remaining pitta rounds to soften, then repeat with remaining lamb filling and more oil spray.

5 Tops pies with hummus, fetta and chopped parsley; serve with lemon wedges.

BEEF & ALE PIE FLOATER

PREP + COOK TIME
1 HOUR

MAKES 10

3 sheets frozen shortcrust pastry, thawed

3 sheets frozen puff pastry, thawed

1 egg, beaten lightly

BEEF ALE FILLING

1 medium onion (150g)

1 medium carrot (120g)

2 cloves garlic

650g (1¼lb) porterhouse steak

2 tablespoons olive oil

2 tablespoons plain flour (all-purpose flour)

1½ cups (375ml) pale ale

½ cup (125ml) beef stock

1 tablespoon tomato paste

1 tablespoon thyme leaves

PEA FLOATER

375g (12oz) frozen peas

½ cup (120g) crème fraîche

1 tablespoon chopped mint

2 teaspoons lemon juice

1 To make beef ale filling, finely chop onion, carrot and garlic. Cut steak into 2cm (¾in) pieces. Heat 1 tablespoon oil in a large heavy-based saucepan over a high heat; cook beef in batches, until browned. Transfer to a plate. Heat remaining oil in same pan; cook onion, carrot and garlic, stirring, for 5 minutes or until softened. Stir in resting juices from beef then flour until mixture bubbles. Add ale, stock, tomato paste and thyme; bring to the boil. Reduce heat; simmer, covered, for 10 minutes. Remove lid; simmer for 5 minutes or until sauce is thickened. Add beef back to pan; simmer, uncovered, for 1 minute. Season. Cool. (Makes 2⅔ cups.)

2 Lightly grease and preheat a 4-hole (⅓-cup/80ml) pie maker.

3 Using pastry cutter provided, cut 10 large rounds (11cm/4½in) from shortcrust pastry and 10 small rounds (9.5cm/4in) from puff pastry. Line prepared holes with shortcrust pastry rounds, pressing into base and sides. Refrigerate remaining pastry rounds until required.

4 Spoon ¼ cup beef ale filling into each pastry case. Top with puff pastry rounds; press edges firmly to seal. Brush with egg. Close lid; cook for 8 minutes or until pastry is golden. Remove pies; transfer to a wire rack. Repeat in batches with remaining pastry rounds, beef ale filling and egg to make 10 pies in total.

5 To make pea floater, place frozen peas in a heatproof bowl, cover with boiling water; stand for 1 minute. Drain. Process peas, crème fraîche, mint and lemon in a food processor until coarsely chopped, season to taste. (Makes 2 cups.)

6 Serve pies on pea floater.

CHICKEN CURRY RICE CRUST PIE

PREP + COOK TIME
50 MINUTES

MAKES 6

250g (8oz) packet microwave brown rice and quinoa

2 eggs

cooking oil spray

2 sheets frozen puff pastry, thawed

CURRY FILLING

1 tablespoon olive oil

4 green onions (scallions), sliced thinly

2 tablespoons panang curry paste

400g (12½oz) chicken thigh fillets, cut into 2cm (¾in) pieces

2 kaffir lime leaves, shredded finely

⅔ cup (160g) coconut cream

1 teaspoon fish sauce

1 To make curry filling, heat oil in a medium saucepan over medium heat; cook green onion, stirring, for 1 minute. Add curry paste and chicken; cook until browned. Stir in lime leaves and coconut cream; bring to the boil. Reduce heat to low-medium, cook for 10 minutes or until chicken is cooked though and sauce is thickened. Stir in fish sauce. Cool. (Makes 1½ cups.)

2 Process brown rice and quinoa with 1 egg until finely ground but not a paste. (Makes 1 cup.)

3 Generously spray a 2-hole (100ml) pie maker with oil. Using pastry cutter provided, cut six small rounds (9.5cm/4in) from puff pastry. Refrigerate pastry rounds until required.

4 Place 2 rounded tablespoons rice mixture into each hole; press firmly into base and side using the back of a spoon. Turn pie maker on. Close lid; cook for 3 minutes until firm.

5 Spoon ¼ cup curry filling into each rice case. Top with puff pastry rounds; press edges firmly to seal. Lightly beat remaining egg; brush over pastry. Close lid; cook for 7 minutes or until pastry is golden. Remove pies; transfer to a wire rack. Repeat in batches with remaining rice mixture, curry filling, pastry rounds and beaten egg to make six in total.

COOK'S NOTE

Cooked pastizzi can be frozen for up to 2 months. Thaw in the fridge overnight. Reheat in the pie maker for 8 minutes.

THREE CHEESE PASTIZZI

PREP + COOK TIME
35 MINUTES

MAKES 8

½ cup (120g) firm ricotta, crumbled

½ cup (50g) coarsely grated haloumi

¼ cup (20g) finely grated parmesan

¼ teaspoon dried chilli flakes

1 teaspoon finely grated lemon rind

1 teaspoon lemon juice

2 tablespoons finely chopped mint

2 sheets frozen puff pastry, thawed

1 egg yolk

1½ tablespoons sesame seeds

lemon wedges, to serve

1 Combine ricotta, haloumi, parmesan, chili flakes, lemon rind and juice, and mint in a small bowl. Season. (Makes 1¼ cups.)

2 Lightly grease and preheat a 4-hole (⅓-cup/80ml) pie maker.

3 Cut eight 7cm (2¾in) rounds from each puff pastry sheet; you will have 16 rounds. Place 1 heaped tablespoon of cheese mixture in the centre of eight pastry rounds. Place a second round of pastry over filling to enclose. Using a fork, crimp around the edge of each round to seal. Combine egg yolk and 1 teaspoon water in a small bowl; brush egg wash on pies. Sprinkle with the sesame seeds.

4 Place four pastries into prepared holes. Close lid; cook for 10 minutes. Turn over; cook a further 3 minutes or until golden. Remove pastries; transfer to a wire rack. Repeat with remaining pastries.

5 Serve pastizzi straightaway with lemon wedges.

BRIE & FIG PIES

PREP + COOK TIME
30 MINUTES

MAKES 10

- **⅔ cup (220g) fig jam**
- **2 tablespoons coarsely chopped walnuts**
- **3 sheets frozen puff pastry, thawed**
- **10 slices prosciutto (150g), halved**
- **300g (9½oz) brie, cut into 20 squares**
- **5 small fresh figs, halved**
- **1 tablespoon lemon thyme leaves**

1 Combine jam and walnuts in a small bowl.

2 Lightly grease and preheat a 4-hole (⅓-cup/80ml) pie maker.

3 Using pastry cutter provided, cut 10 large rounds (11cm/4½in) from puff pastry. Line prepared holes with pastry rounds, pressing into base and sides. Refrigerate remaining pastry rounds until required.

4 Place 2 prosciutto halves in each pastry case; top with 1 tablespoon jam mixture, 2 squares of brie and a fig half (or 2 quarters depending on the size of the figs). Sprinkle with thyme leaves. Close lid; cook for 9 minutes or until pastry is golden brown. Remove pies; transfer to a wire rack. Repeat in batches with remaining pastry rounds, prosciutto, jam mixture, brie squares and figs to make 10 pies in total.

5 Serve pies straightaway.

COOK'S NOTE

You can make these pies with dried figs or wedges of fresh apricot. Brie can be swapped out for camembert, goat's cheese or blue cheese.

MINI BEEF WELLINGTONS

PREP + COOK TIME
35 MINUTES
(+ COOLING)

MAKES 4

2 tablespoons olive oil
2 x 150g (4½oz) beef eye-fillet
4 cap mushrooms (20g), stalks trimmed
2 teaspoons dijon mustard
1 teaspoon finely chopped thyme leaves
2 tablespoons mushroom dip
4 slices prosciutto (60g)
1 sheet frozen shortcrust pastry, thawed
8 small thyme sprigs
gravy, to serve

1 Heat 1 tablespoon of the oil in a large frying pan; cook steaks for 2 minutes each side. Remove from pan. Cool. Add remaining oil to pan; cook mushrooms 1 minute each side. Cut steaks in half for four pieces.

2 Spread ½ teaspoon mustard on each piece of steak; sprinkle each with ¼ teaspoon thyme then top with 2 teaspoons mushroom dip. Wrap a slice of prosciutto around each piece of steak.

3 Lightly grease and preheat a 2-hole (100ml) pie maker.

4 Cut pastry into four squares. Place a prosciutto-wrapped steak in the centre of a pastry square; sit a mushroom on top, stalk-side down. Lift pastry edges up to cover the steak leaving the mushroom cap exposed. Top mushroom cap with thyme sprigs.

5 Place beef wellingtons into prepared holes. Close lid; cook for 6 minutes or until browned.

6 Serve wellingtons with gravy.

ONE-HANDED BREAKFAST PIES

PREP + COOK TIME
15 MINUTES

MAKES 4

4 frozen hash browns (72g each)

2 pieces medium-thick sliced ham (100g)

4 eggs (50g each)

cooking oil spray

spicy tomato relish and chives, to serve

1 Defrost hash browns in the microwave using DEFROST setting for 1½ minutes.

2 Place hash browns in an ungreased 4-hole (⅓-cup/80ml) pie maker, pressing into the base and up the side of each hole to form a case. Season. Close lid; cook for 5 minutes or until potato case is crisp.

3 Using the pastry cutter provided cut four small rounds (9.5cm/4in) from ham. Reserve scraps for another use.

4 Crack an egg into a small cup. Open pie maker. Carefully tip the egg into the potato case. Place ham round over egg and spray with a little oil. Repeat filling with remaining eggs and ham. Close lid; cook for 6 minutes, then cook for a further 1 minute with the lid open, or until whites are set but yolks are only just set, or until egg is cooked as desired.

5 Carefully lift pies out with a spoon. Serve straightaway topped with tomato relish and chives.

CREAM OF MUSHROOM SOUP PIES

PREP + COOK TIME
30 MINUTES
(+ COOLING)

MAKES 8

2 sheets frozen shortcrust pastry, thawed
2 sheets frozen puff pastry, thawed
3 sprigs thyme
1 egg, beaten lightly

MUSHROOM SOUP FILLING

1 tablespoon olive oil
1 large onion (150g), chopped finely
40g (1½oz) butter
350g (11oz) small button mushrooms, quartered
1 teaspoon thyme leaves
2 cloves garlic, chopped finely
420g (13½oz) can cream of mushroom soup

1 To make mushroom soup filling, heat the oil in a large frying pan over high heat; cook onion for 5 minutes or until softened. Add butter; once melted, add mushrooms, thyme and garlic then cook, stirring, for 5 minutes or until mushrooms are browned. Add mushroom soup and 2 tablespoons water; cook, stirring, for 5 minutes or until thickened. Season if necessary. Cool.

2 Lightly grease and preheat a 4-hole (⅓-cup/80ml) pie maker.

3 Using pastry cutter provided, cut eight large rounds (11cm/4½in) from shortcrust pastry and eight small rounds (9.5cm/4in) from puff pastry. Line prepared holes with shortcrust pastry rounds, pressing into base and side. Refrigerate remaining pastry rounds until required.

4 Spoon ¼ cup mushroom soup filling into each pastry case. Top with puff pastry rounds; press edges firmly to seal. Brush pastry with egg. Close lid; cook for 7 minutes or until pastry is golden. Remove pies; transfer to a wire rack. Repeat with remaining pastry rounds, mushroom soup filling and egg.

tip Use the puff pastry offcuts to stamp out the letter M (as pictured) or other desired decorative shapes. Position on pies before brushing with egg.

REALLY GOOD CHICKEN PIES

PREP + COOK TIME
45 MINUTES

MAKES 10

3 sheets frozen shortcrust pastry, thawed

3 sheets frozen puff pastry, thawed

1 egg, beaten lightly

CHICKEN FILLING

150g (4½oz) asparagus, chopped into 2cm (¾in) pieces

60g (2oz) butter

1 large leek (500g), sliced thinly

2 stalks celery (300g), trimmed, chopped finely

2 cloves garlic, crushed

½ cup finely chopped tarragon leaves, plus 10 sprigs extra to decorate

50g (1½oz) pancetta, chopped finely

1½ tablespoons plain flour (all-purpose flour)

1 tablespoon dijon mustard

½ cup (125ml) chicken stock

200ml crème fraîche

2 cups (320g) shredded cooked chicken

1 To make chicken filling, pour boiling water over asparagus in a medium heatproof bowl; stand for 2 minutes, drain. Heat butter in a large saucepan; cook leek, celery and garlic, stirring, until softened. Add tarragon; cook for 5 minutes. Stir in pancetta; cook, stirring, for 5 minutes or until crisp. Stir flour into mixture; cook for 2 minutes. Stir in mustard, stock and crème fraîche, simmer until mixture thickens. Season. Stir in chicken and asparagus. (Makes 3 cups.)

2 Lightly grease and preheat a 4-hole (⅓-cup/80ml) pie maker.

3 Using pastry cutter provided, cut ten large rounds (11cm/4½in) from shortcrust pastry and ten small rounds (9.5cm/4in) from puff pastry. Line prepared holes with shortcrust pastry rounds, pressing into base and side. Refrigerate remaining pastry rounds until required.

4 Spoon heaped ¼ cup chicken filling into each pastry case. Top with puff pastry rounds; press edges firmly to seal. Place 1 tarragon sprig on each pie; brush top of pies with egg. Close lid; cook for 8 minutes or until pastry is golden. Remove pies; transfer to a wire rack. Repeat in batches with remaining pastry rounds, chicken filling, tarragon sprigs and egg to make 10 pies in total.

COOK'S NOTE

Chicken pies can be frozen for up to 3 months. Thaw in fridge overnight. Reheat in the pie maker for 12 minutes.

COOK'S NOTE

To make these in a smaller pie maker, see page 7 for information on how much filling they hold, then adjust accordingly. Pies can be frozen for up to 3 months.

KOREAN BEEF SHORT RIB PIES

PREP + COOK TIME
1 HOUR 45 MINUTES

MAKES 6

½ cup (100g) kimchi, plus extra to serve

1½ cup (300g) frozen podded edamame (soy beans), boiled

6 sheets frozen shortcrust pastry, thawed

2 sheets frozen puff pastry, thawed

1 egg, beaten lightly

BEEF RIB FILLING

¾ cup (180ml) salt-reduced beef stock

½ cup (125ml) salt-reduced soy sauce

2 tablespoons oyster sauce

¼ cup (60ml) worcestershire sauce

1 tablespoon sriracha

4 cloves garlic, chopped finely

2 tablespoons finely grated ginger

4 green onions (scallions), cut into 3cm (1¼in) pieces

1.4kg (3¾lb) beef short ribs, cut into 6 ribs

1 To make beef rib filling, combine all ingredients, except beef ribs in a 6-litre (24-cup) electric pressure cooker. Lay ribs flat, side-by-side in the cooker. Bring cooker to high pressure. Release pressure; cook for 1 hour. Remove ribs; simmer cooking liquid until reduce to 1 cup. Remove meat from bones in chunks; place in a medium bowl.

2 Strain reduced cooking liquid. Add ½ cup with strained solids to beef chunks with kimchi and 1 cup of the edamame; stir to combine. Cool. (Makes 4 cups.)

3 Lightly grease and preheat a 4-hole (¾-cup/180ml) pie maker.

4 Using pastry cutter provided, cut six large rounds (15.5cm/6¼in) from shortcrust pastry and six small rounds (12cm/4¾in) from puff pastry. Line prepared holes with shortcrust pastry rounds, pressing into base and side. Refrigerate remaining pastry rounds until required.

5 Spoon ⅔ cup firmly packed beef rib filling into each pastry case. Top with puff pastry rounds; press edges firmly to seal. Brush pastry with egg. Close lid; cook for 9 minutes or until pastry is golden. Remove pies; transfer to a wire rack. Repeat with remaining pastry rounds, beef rib filling and egg.

6 Serve pies topped with remaining edamame and extra kimchi.

LAMB RAGU PIES WITH GNOCCHI

PREP + COOK TIME
50 MINUTES

MAKES 16

500g (1lb) bought baby gnocchi

50g (1½oz) butter, melted

⅓ cup (25g) grated parmesan

4 sheets frozen shortcrust pastry, thawed

LAMB RAGU FILLING

2 tablespoons olive oil

650g (1¼lb) lamb back strap, cut into 2cm (¾in) pieces

1 small onion (80g), chopped finely

1 medium carrot (120g), chopped finely

1 stalk celery (150g), chopped finely

2 cloves garlic, crushed

2 teaspoons finely chopped rosemary

2 tablespoons plain flour (all-purpose flour)

½ cup (125ml) red wine

1½ cups (375ml) beef stock

1 tablespoon tomato paste

1 To make lamb ragu filling, heat 1 tablespoon of the oil in a large heavy-based saucepan over a high heat; cook lamb, in batches, until browned. Transfer to a plate. Heat remaining oil in pan; cook onion, carrot, celery, garlic and rosemary until softened. Stir in lamb resting juices, then flour until mixture bubbles. Stir in wine, stock and tomato paste; bring to the boil. Reduce heat; simmer for 5 minutes or until sauce thickens slightly. Add lamb back to pan, then simmer for 1 minute. Season to taste. Cool. (Makes 4 cups.)

2 Combine gnocchi, butter and parmesan in a large bowl; season.

3 Lightly grease and preheat a 4-hole (⅓-cup/80ml) pie maker.

4 Using pastry cutter provided, cut 16 large rounds (11cm/4½in) from shortcrust pastry. Line prepared holes with pastry rounds, pressing into the base and side. Refrigerate remaining pastry rounds until required.

5 Spoon ¼ cup filling into each pastry case. Cover filling with 1½ tablespoons gnocchi mixture. Close lid; cook for 5 minutes or until golden. Remove pies; transfer to a wire rack.Repeat in batches with remaining pastry rounds, lamb ragu filling and gnocchi mixture to make 16 pies in total.

COOK'S NOTE

You could also use 300g (9½oz) leftover cooked spaghetti and 16 meatballs and sauce (2 cups).

SPAGHETTI & MEATBALL PIES

PREP + COOK TIME
40 MINUTES

MAKES 8

150g (4½oz) spaghetti

1 tablespoon olive oil

¾ cup (75g) grated mozzarella

16 bought uncooked meatballs (320g)

500g (1lb) jar tomato pasta sauce

2 tablespoons chopped oregano

2 sheets frozen shortcrust pastry, thawed

2 tablespoons grated parmesan, plus extra to serve

1 Break spaghetti in half; cook in a large saucepan of boiling salted water for 8 minutes or until al dente. Drain. Return to pan with 2 teaspoons olive oil and ½ cup mozzarella, tossing until cheese is melted. Season.

2 Meanwhile, for meatball filling, heat remaining olive oil in a large deep frying pan over medium heat; cook meatballs for 5 minutes until browned. Add pasta sauce and oregano; cook a further 5 minutes. Add remaining mozzarella; stir until melted. Cool. (Makes 2 cups)

3 Lightly grease and preheat a 4-hole (⅓-cup/80ml) pie maker.

4 Using pastry cutter provided, cut eight large rounds (11cm/4½in) from shortcrust pastry. Line prepared holes with pastry rounds, pressing into base and side.

5 Spoon ¼ cup meatball filling (2 meatballs and some sauce) into each pastry case. Top with one eighth of the spaghetti mixture and 1 teaspoon parmesan. Close lid; cook for 6 minutes or until golden. Remove pies; transfer to a wire rack. Repeat with remaining pastry rounds, meatball filling, spaghetti mixture and parmesan.

6 Serve pies topped with extra grated parmesan.

SWEET AS PIE

S'MORES

PREP + COOK TIME
40 MINUTES

MAKES 8

125g (4oz) digestive biscuits

60g (2oz) butter, melted

3 sheets frozen shortcrust pastry, thawed

100g (3oz) white marshmallows

180g (5½oz) dark (semi-sweet) chocolate, chopped very coarsely

1 Place biscuits in a zip-top bag; seal bag. Using the palm of your hand or a rolling pin, crush biscuits into pieces. Add melted butter to bag; seal bag. Massage bag until combined. (Makes ½ cup.)

2 Lightly grease and preheat a 4-hole (⅓-cup/80ml) pie maker.

3 Using pastry cutter provided, cut out eight large rounds (11cm/4½in) from shortcrust pastry. Line prepared holes with pastry rounds, pressing into the base and side. Refrigerate remaining pastry rounds until required.

4 Close lid; cook for 5 minutes or until pastry is golden. Remove pastry cases; transfer to a wire rack. Repeat with remaining pastry rounds. Cool.

5 Divide half the marshmallows among pastry cases, flatten to cover bases. Top each with an eighth of the chocolate then remaining marshmallows.

6 Place four filled cases back in pie maker. Place a wooden spoon or other 2cm (¾in) object on the edge of the pie maker to keep the lid slightly ajar. Partially close lid; cook for 9 minutes or until chocolate is melted. Top s'mores with half the biscuit mixture; partially close lid held slightly ajar, for a further 2 minutes. Remove s'mores; transfer to a wire rack to cool. Repeat cooking with remaining filled cases and biscuit mixture.

WHOLE MANDARIN ALMOND PIES

PREP + COOK TIME
1 HOUR 30 MINUTES

MAKES 6

2 mandarins (210g)

2 eggs

¼ cup (55g) caster sugar (superfine sugar)

¼ teaspoon baking powder

1 cup (120g) almond meal

2 sheets frozen butter puff pastry, thawed

6 dehydrated blood orange or orange slices

¼ cup (85g) orange marmalade, warmed

½ cup (40g) flaked almonds, toasted

1 Place whole mandarins in a large saucepan and cover with water; bring to the boil. Reduce heat to medium; simmer for 1 hour or until very soft. Drain. When cool enough to handle, cut in half and remove any pips. Gently squeeze mandarin halves to remove excess liquid but do not squeeze dry. Place mandarin halves in a food processor, with skin intact; process to a puree. Add eggs, sugar, baking powder and almond meal; process until combined. (Makes 1½ cups.)

2 Preheat a 4-hole (⅓-cup/80ml) pie maker.

3 Using pastry cutter provided, cut six large rounds (11cm/4½in) from puff pastry. Line pie maker holes with pastry rounds, pressing into base and side. Refigerate remaining pastry rounds until required.

4 Spoon ¼ cup mandarin filling into each pastry case and top with a blood orange slice. Close lid; cook for 13 minutes or until pastry is golden and cake centre is firm to the touch. Remove pies; transfer to a wire rack. Repeat with remaining pastry rounds, mandarin filling and blood orange slices.

5 Brush hot pies wth marmalade. Serve topped with almonds.

PEAR & DULCE DE LECHE PIES

PREP + COOK TIME
30 MINUTES

MAKES 8

400g (12½oz) can pear slices in juice, drained

2 sheets frozen shortcrust pastry, thawed

2 sheets frozen puff pastry, thawed

⅔ cup (200g) dulce de leche

2 tablespoons hazelnut meal

1 egg, beaten lightly

1 Pat pear slices well with paper towel to absorb any moisture.

2 Lightly grease and preheat a 4-hole (⅓-cup/80ml) pie maker.

3 Using pastry cutter provided, cut out eight large rounds (11cm/4½in) from shortcrust pastry and eight small rounds (9.5cm/4in) from puff pastry. Using the puff pastry off cuts, cut out eight letter P shapes, or decoration of choice, using the point of a small sharp knife. Line prepared holes with shortcrust pastry rounds, pressing into the base and side. Refrigerate remaining pastry rounds and shapes until required.

4 Spoon 1 tablespoon dulce de leche into each pastry case. Sprinkle each with 1 teaspoon hazelnut meal. Arrange 3 pear slices over the base. Top with puff pastry rounds; press edges firmly to seal. Place pastry P shapes on top; brush with egg. Close lid; cook for 8 minutes or until golden. Remove pies; transfer to a wire rack. Repeat with remaining pastry rounds, dulce de leche, hazelnut meal, pear and egg.

PEAR & HAZELNUT FRANGIPANE PIES

PREP + COOK TIME
40 MINUTES

MAKES 6

125g (4oz) butter, softened

½ cup (110g) caster sugar (superfine sugar)

⅓ cup (110g) lime marmalade

1 teaspoon vanilla extract

2 eggs

¾ cup (75g) hazelnut meal

2 tablespoons plain flour (all-purpose flour)

3 mini pears (100g each)

1½ sheets frozen shortcrust pastry, thawed

roasted chopped hazelnuts, to serve

1 To make frangipane, beat butter, sugar, 2 tablespoons lime marmalade and the vanilla in a small bowl with an electric mixer until light and fluffy. Beat in eggs, one at a time. Fold in hazelnut meal and flour. (Makes 1½ cups.)

2 Cut two cross-section slices from the centre of each pear. Reserve remaining pears for another use.

3 Lightly grease and preheat a 4-hole (⅓-cup/80ml) pie maker.

4 Using pastry cutter provided, cut six large rounds (11cm/4½in) from shortcrust pastry. Line prepared holes with pastry rounds, pressing into the base and side. Refrigerate remaining rounds until required.

5 Spoon ¼ cup frangipane into pastry cases; smooth surface. Place a pear slice on top. Place a wooden spoon or other 2cm (¾in) object on the edge of the pie maker to keep the lid slightly ajar. Partially close lid; cook for 12 minutes.

6 Heat remaining marmalade in a small microwave-safe bowl in the microwave on HIGH (100%) for 20 seconds until melted. Brush tops of the pies. Partially close lid; cook for a further 2 minutes or until a skewer inserted into the centre of a pie comes out clean. Remove pies; transfer to a wire rack.

7 Repeat steps 5 and 6 with remaining pastry rounds, frangipane and pear slices, then brush with remaining marmalade.

8 Serve pies topped with chopped hazelnuts.

STRAWBERRY POP TARTS

PREP + COOK TIME
35 MINUTES

MAKES 4

2 sheets frozen shortcrust pastry, thawed

60g (2oz) shortbread biscuits, crushed

1 cup (160g) icing sugar (confectioners' sugar)

1 tablespoon buttermilk

2 drops pink colouring

2 teaspoons unicorn confetti

STRAWBERRY FILLING

200g (6½oz) strawberries, chopped coarsely

¼ cup (80g) strawberry jam

1 teaspoon caster sugar (superfine sugar)

½ teaspoon vanilla bean paste

1 teaspoon cornflour (cornstarch)

1 To make strawberry filling, place ingredients in a small saucepan; cook, stirring occasionally, over medium heat for 12 minutes or until mixture boils and thickens. Cool. (Makes 1 cup.)

2 Lightly grease and preheat a 4-hole (⅓-cup/80ml) pie maker.

3 Using pastry cutter provided, cut four large rounds (11cm/4½in) and four small rounds (9.5cm/4in) from shortcrust pastry. Line prepared holes with large pastry rounds, pressing into base and side.

4 Spoon ¼ cup strawberry filling into pastry cases, sprinkle each with 1½ tablespoons biscuit crumbs then top with small pastry rounds; press edges firmly to seal. Close lid; cook for 10 minutes or until golden brown. Cool slightly.

5 Stir sifted icing sugar, buttermilk and food colouring in a small bowl until smooth. Spread icing on pop tarts, then top with confetti.

MISO CARAMEL APPLE PIES

PREP + COOK TIME
25 MINUTES

MAKES 4

385g (12oz) can pie apple slices

1 tablespoon white (shiro) miso

¼ cup (55g) caster sugar (superfine sugar)

½ teaspoon ground cinnamon

¼ teaspoon ground ginger

1 sheet frozen shortcrust pastry, thawed

2 small red apples (100g)

MISO CARAMEL

½ cup (150g) canned caramel top 'n' fill

2 tablespoons white (shiro) miso

1 Drain canned apple slices over a small bowl; reserve 1½ tablespoons liquid, then discard remainder. Combine reserved liquid with miso in a medium bowl; fold through drained apple, 2 tablespoons of the caster sugar, ¼ teaspoon cinnamon and the ginger. (Makes 1⅓ cups).

2 Lightly grease and preheat a 4-hole (⅓-cup/80ml) pie maker.

3 Using pastry cutter provided, cut four large rounds (11cm/4½in) from shortcrust pastry. Line prepared holes with pastry rounds, pressing into base and side.

4 Spoon ⅓ cup apple mixture into pastry cases. Cut apples into quarters; remove core, cut into 2mm (1/12in) thin slices. Arrange in a spiral pattern over each pie. Combine remaining sugar and cinnamon, then sprinkle each pie with ½ teaspoon. Close lid; cook for 5 minutes or until golden.

5 Meanwhile, to make miso caramel, heat caramel top 'n' fill in a small microwave-safe bowl in the microwave on HIGH (100%) for 40 seconds until melted. Whisk through the miso until smooth.

6 Serve pies warm sprinkled with remaining cinnamon sugar and drizzled with miso caramel sauce.

BLUEBERRY COBBLER PIES

PREP + COOK TIME
35 MINUTES

MAKES 8

1 cup (150g) self-raising flour

2 teaspoons baking powder

1½ tablespoons caster sugar (superfine sugar)

50g (1½oz) butter, softened

¾ cup (180ml) buttermilk

2 cups (300g) fresh or frozen blueberries, thawed

1 tablespoon lemon juice

2 teaspoons cornflour (cornstarch)

1 teaspoon vanilla bean paste

2 sheets frozen shortcrust pastry, thawed

icing sugar (confectioners' sugar) and thick (double) cream, to serve

1 Sift flour, baking powder and 1 tablespoon of the sugar into a small bowl; rub in butter with your fingertips. Make a well in the centre; add buttermilk, stir to form a soft and sticky dough.

2 Combine blueberries, remaining sugar, lemon juice, cornflour and vanilla in a small bowl. Strain any juices left in the bowl.

3 Lightly grease and preheat a 4-hole (⅓-cup/80ml) pie maker.

4 Using pastry cutter provided, cut eight large rounds (11cm/4½in) from shortcrust pastry. Line prepared holes with pastry rounds, pressing into base and side. Refrigerate remaining rounds until required.

5 Spoon 2 tablespoons blueberry mixture into each pastry case; top with a scant 2 tablespoons dough mixture, flatten slightly with a spoon. Close lid; cook for 7 minutes. Lift lid; place a wooden spoon or other 2cm (¾in) object on the edge of the pie maker to keep the lid slightly ajar. Partially close lid; cook for a further 3 minutes or until tops are golden. Remove pies; transfer to a wire rack. Repeat with remaining pastry rounds, blueberry mixture and dough mixture.

6 Serve pies warm dusted with icing sugar and topped with cream.

COOK'S NOTE

Replace Fruit Loops with Coco Pops, Cornflakes or Crunchy Nut cereal.

CEREAL MILK CUSTARD TARTS

PREP + COOK TIME
35 MINUTES
(+ REFRIGERATION)

MAKES 8

395g (12½oz) can sweetened condensed milk

2 cups (500ml) thickened cream (heavy cream)

1½ cups (60g) Fruit Loops, plus extra to serve

2 tablespoons cornflour (cornstarch)

1 teaspoon soft butter

2 sheets frozen shortcrust pastry, thawed

1 Whisk condensed milk and 1¾ cups (430ml) cream in a medium saucepan over medium heat until combined. Add cereal; cook, stirring, for 5 minutes to flavour milk mixture. Strain over a bowl; discard cereal. Return milk mixture to pan. Combine cornflour and remaining cream; whisk into milk mixture over medium heat for 5 minutes or until mixture boils and thickens. Stir in butter; cool completely. (Makes 2 cups.)

2 Lightly grease and preheat a 4-hole (⅓-cup/80ml) pie maker.

3 Using pastry cutter provided, cut eight large rounds (11cm/4½in) from shortcrust pastry. Line prepared holes with pastry rounds, pressing into base and side.

4 Close lid; cook for 2 minutes or until pastry is golden. Remove tart cases; transfer to a wire rack. Repeat with remaining pastry rounds. Cool.

5 Place cooled tart cases on a tray. Spoon a scant ¼ cup custard filling into each; smooth the surface.

6 Place four filled tart cases back in pie maker. Close lid; cook for 15 minutes or until custard is set with a wobble. Remove tarts; transfer to a wire rack. Repeat with remaining filled tart cases. Cool. Refrierate for 30 minutes.

7 Serve custard tarts topped with extra cereal.

PINA COLADA PIES

PREP + COOK TIME
40 MINUTES

MAKES 6

1½ sheets frozen shortcrust pastry, thawed

6 caramel stroopwafels (187g)

icing sugar (confectioners' sugar), to dust

PINA COLADA FILLING

425g (13½oz) can pineapple pieces in syrup

2 tablespoons rum

¼ cup (90g) dulce de leche

2 egg yolks

¼ cup (20g) shredded coconut, toasted

1 To make pina colada filling, drain canned pineapple pieces over a small bowl; reserve syrup. Pat pineappple dry with paper towel. Place reserved syrup, rum, dulce de leche and egg yolks in a medium saucepan; whisk over low heat for 5 minutes until mixture thickens enough to coat the back of a spoon. Remove from heat; stir through pineapple and coconut. Cool. (Makes 1½ cups.)

2 Lightly grease and preheat a 4-hole (⅓-cup/80ml) pie maker.

3 Using pastry cutter provided, cut six large rounds (11cm/4½in) from shortcrust pastry. Line prepared holes with pastry rounds, pressing into base and side. Refrigerate remaining rounds until required.

4 Spoon ¼ cup pina colada filling into pastry cases. Cover each with a stroopwafel. Close lid; cook for 8 minutes or until golden. Remove pies; transfer to a wire rack. Repeat with remaining pastry rounds, pina colada filling and stroopwafels.

5 Serve pies warm dusted with icing sugar.

OREO PUDDING PIES

PREP + COOK TIME
40 MINUTES

MAKES 4

1 sheet frozen shortcrust pastry, thawed

½ cup (125g) bought vanilla frosting

CHOCOLATE FILLING

50g (1½oz) butter, chopped

50g (1½oz) dark (semi-sweet) chocolate, chopped coarsely

¼ cup (55g) firmly packed brown sugar

1 egg, beaten lightly

¼ cup (35g) plain flour (all-purpose flour)

2 teaspoons cocoa powder

2 x 23g (¾oz) bags mini Oreos, chopped coarsely, plus extra to serve

1 To make chocolate filling, place butter and chocolate in a saucepan over low heat; cook, stirring, for 5 minutes or until melted and smooth. Remove from heat. Stir in sugar, then egg; mix well. Sift flour and cocoa powder over chocolate mixture. Add chopped biscuits; stir until combined. (Makes ¾ cup.)

2 Lightly grease and preheat a 4-hole (⅓-cup/80ml) pie maker.

3 Using pastry cutter provided, cut four large rounds (11cm/4½in) from shortcrust pastry. Line prepared holes with pastry rounds, pressing into base and side.

4 Pour chocolate filling evenly into pastry cases. Close lid; cook for 10 minutes or until filling is risen and firm to touch. Remove pies; transfer to a wire rack to cool completely.

5 To serve, spoon frosting on pies; top with extra chopped biscuits.

RHUBARB RICE PUDDING PIES

PREP + COOK TIME
30 MINUTES

MAKES 6

2 sheets frozen shortcrust pastry, thawed

2 sheets frozen puff pastry, thawed

420g (13½oz) can creamed rice

1 egg, beaten lightly

maple syrup, to serve

RHUBARB FILLING

400g (12½oz) trimmed rhubarb stalks, cut into 2cm (¾in) pieces

½ cup (110g) caster sugar (superfine sugar)

⅓ cup (80ml) orange juice

1 To make rhubarb filling, combine rhubarb, sugar and orange juice in a medium saucepan; stir over high heat for 6 minutes until rhubarb is tender. (Makes 1¾ cups.)

2 Lightly grease and preheat a 4-hole (⅓-cup/80ml) pie maker.

3 Using pastry cutter provided, cut six large rounds (11cm/4½in) from shortcrust pastry and six small rounds (9.5cm/4in) from puff pastry. (Keep pastry scraps for another use; see page 157.)

4 Line prepared holes with shortcrust pastry rounds, press into base and side. Refrigerate remaining rounds until required. Close lid; cook for 2 minutes or until light golden. Remove pastry cases; transfer to a wire rack. Repeat with remaining shortcrust pastry rounds.

5 Spoon a scant ¼ cup creamed rice into each pastry case, followed by 2 tablespoons rhubarb filing (you will have 2 tablespoons creamed rice leftover). Top with puff pastry rounds, pressing gently around the edge to seal. Brush tops with egg.

6 Place four pies back in the pie maker. Close lid; cook for 8 minutes or until golden. Remove pies; transfer to a wire rack. Repeat with remaining pies.

7 Serves pies warm drizzled with maple syrup.

COOK'S NOTE

Any leftover rhubarb will keep refrigerated for up to 3 days or frozen for 1 month.

PB&J PIES

PREP + COOK TIME
40 MINUTES

MAKES 6

1½ sheets frozen shortcrust pastry, thawed

¼ cup (80g) raspberry jam, plus extra to serve

2 tablespoons smooth peanut butter

85g (3oz) dark (semi-sweet) chocolate, melted

FRANGIPANE

100g (3oz) butter, softened

½ cup (110g) caster sugar (superfine sugar)

1 teaspoon vanilla extract

2 eggs

¾ cup (90g) almond meal

2 tablespoons plain flour (all-purpose flour)

⅓ cup (60g) Reese's Peanut Butter Chips

1 To make frangipane, beat butter, sugar and vanilla in a small bowl with an electric mixer until light and fluffy. Beat in eggs, one at a time. Fold in almond meal, flour and peanut butter chips. (Makes 1½ cups.)

2 Lightly grease and preheat a 4-hole (⅓-cup/80ml) pie maker.

3 Using pastry cutter provided, cut six large rounds (11cm/4½in) from shortcrust pastry. Line prepared holes with pastry rounds, pressing into the base and side. Refrigerate remaining rounds until required.

4 Spoon 2 teaspoons jam into each pastry case, then add ¼ cup frangipane mixture; smooth surface. Close lid; cook for 14 minutes or until a skewer inserted into the centre of one pie comes out clean. Remove pies; transfer to a wire rack. Repeat with remaining pastry rounds, jam and frangipane.

5 Place peanut butter in a small micrwave-safe cup. Microwave on LOW (50%) for 15 seconds or until runny. Swirl peanut butter through melted chocolate.

6 Serve pies topped with extra jam and the peanut butter mixture.

HOT CROSS BUN APPLE PIES

PREP + COOK TIME
40 MINUTES

MAKES 6

6 fruit hot cross buns (480g)

50g (2½oz) butter, softened

2 tablespoons cinnamon sugar

385g (12oz) can pie apples, drained

2 tablespoons caster sugar (superfine sugar)

vanilla custard, to serve

1 Preheat a 4-hole (⅓-cup/80ml) pie maker.

2 Split hot cross buns horizontally. Using a rolling pin, gently roll bases until 5mm (¼in) thick. Reserve bun tops.

3 Spread half the butter on the outside of the bun bases; sprinkle with half the cinnamon sugar. Line ungreased holes with bun bases, sugar-side down, pressing into the base and side.

4 Combine pie apples and caster sugar in a bowl. Spoon into cases. Spread bun tops with remaining butter then place over apple filling. Sprinkle with remaining cinnamon sugar. Close lid; cook for 5 minutes or until toasted and heated through. Remove pies; transfer to a wire rack. Repeat with remaining sugared bun bases, apple filling, bun tops, butter and cinnamon sugar.

5 Serve pies warm with custard.

LEMON & LIME MERINGUE PIES

PREP + COOK TIME
25 MINUTES

MAKES 4

1 sheet frozen shortcrust pastry, thawed

2 teaspoons finely grated lime rind

⅔ cup (200g) bought lemon curd

4 x 7cm (2¾in) bought meringue nests

whipped cream and passionfruit pulp, to serve

1 Lightly grease and preheat a 4-hole (⅓-cup/80ml) pie maker.

2 Using pastry cutter provided, cut four large rounds (11cm/4½in) from shortcrust pastry. Line prepared holes with pastry rounds, pressing into base and side. Close lid; cook for 5 minutes or until pastry is golden. Remove pastry cases; transfer to a wire rack. Cool.

3 Stir lime rind through lemon curd. Spoon 2 tablespoons curd mixture into each cooled pie case (be careful not to over fill, there should be a 2mm (1/12in) gap below pie rim); smooth the surface.

4 Place filled cases back in pie maker; top with a meringue nest, flat-side down. Close lid without clipping shut; cook for 3 minutes or until meringue is light golden.

5 Serve pies straightaway topped with cream and passionfruit.

APRICOT LATTICE PIE

PREP + COOK TIME
30 MINUTES

MAKES 4

410g (13oz) can apricot halves in juice

½ cup (160g) apricot jam

1 teaspoon ground ginger

½ cup (70g) macadamias, roasted, chopped finely

1 sheet frozen shortcrust pastry, thawed

1 sheet frozen butter puff pastry, thawed

1 egg, beaten lightly

vanilla ice-cream, to serve

1 Drain apricots; place on a tray lined with paper towel, pat dry with more paper towel. Combine jam, ginger and macadamias in a small bowl.

2 Meanwhile, line an oven tray with baking paper. Place shortcrust pastry sheet on a floured surface; cut into 1cm (½in) wide strips. Weave pastry strips on lined tray into a lattice pattern. Freeze for 5 minutes.

3 Lightly grease a 4-hole (⅓-cup/80ml) pie maker.

4 Using pastry cutter provided, cut four large rounds (11cm/4½in) from butter puff pastry and four small rounds (9.5cm/4in) from the lattice shortcrust pastry. With pie maker turned off, line prepared holes with puff pastry rounds, pressing into base and side.

5 Spoon 1½ tablespoons jam mixture into pastry cases, then add 3-4 apricot halves. Cover with a lattice shortcrust round; press edges firmly to seal. Brush lattice with egg. Turn pie maker on. Close lid; cook for 10 minutes or until golden.

6 Serve pies with ice-cream.

EVERYTHING BUT PIE

TRIPLE CHOCOLATE DOUGHNUTS

PREP + COOK TIME
40 MINUTES
(+ STANDING)

MAKES 10

500g (1lb) packet triple-chocolate muffin mix

⅓ cup (80ml) vegetable oil

2 eggs, beaten lightly

200g (6½oz) bought chocolate frosting

sprinkles, cachous, gold leaf, white chocolate stars and icing flowers, to decorate

1 Place muffin mix into a medium bowl with oil, egg and ½ cup (125ml) water; stir until batter is smooth. (Makes 2½ cups.)

2 Lightly grease and preheat a 4-hole (⅓-cup/80ml) pie maker.

3 Pour ¼ cup batter into prepared holes. Close lid; cook for 10 minutes or until a skewer inserted into the centre of a cake comes out clean. Remove cakes; transfer to a wire rack to cool. Repeat in batches with remaining mixture to make 10 cakes in total.

4 Using a small round 2cm (¾in) cutter or apple corer, cut out a hole in the centre of each cake to create a doughnut shape.

5 Place frosting in a microwave-safe bowl; microwave on HIGH (100%) for 30 seconds or until mixture is smooth and runny. Dip tops of doughnuts into frosting then decorate as desired with sprinkles, cachous, gold leaf, white chocolate stars and crushed icing flowers. Stand on wire rack until set.

NUTELLA CHEESECAKE BROWNIES

PREP + COOK TIME
40 MINUTES

MAKES 8

500g (1lb) packet frosted chocolate brownie mix

2 eggs, beaten lightly

125g (4oz) butter, melted

125g (4oz) cream cheese, softened

2 tablespoons Nutella

1 Grease the top side of a 4-hole (⅓-cup/80ml) pie maker; preheat. With 16 paper cases, stack two together to create eight double-layered cases. Place on a tray; spray with oil.

2 Place brownie mix, egg and melted butter in a large bowl; mix with a wooden spoon until combined. Place cream cheese and Nutella in a small bowl; using the end of a teaspoon, mix to just swirl together.

3 Spoon 2 level tablespoons of brownie mixture into each paper case. Top with 1 teaspoon cream cheese mixture. Cover with another 1 tablespoon brownie mixture.

4 Place four brownies in holes. Close lid; cook for 14 minutes or until just set to the touch. Gently remove brownies; transfer to a wire rack to cool. Repeat with remaining brownies.

5 Place frosting from sachet in a microwave-safe bowl; heat on HIGH (100%) for 30 seconds or until runny.

6 Serve warm brownies topped with remaining cream cheese mixture, drizzled with frosting.

RED VELVET LAMINGTONS

PREP + COOK TIME
35 MINUTES

MAKES 10

410g (13oz) packet red velvet cupcake mix

2 eggs

⅔ cup (160ml) milk

60g (2oz) butter, softened

250g (8oz) cream cheese, softened

1 cup (80g) desiccated coconut

1 cup (50g) flaked coconut

½ teaspoon freeze dried strawberry powder (optional)

WHITE CHOCOLATE GLAZE

¾ cup (110g) white Chocolate Melts

30g (1oz) butter

3 cups (480g) icing sugar (confectioners' sugar)

½ cup (125ml) milk

1 Beat cupcake mix, eggs, milk and butter in a large bowl with an electric mixer on low speed until combined. Increase speed to high; beat until smooth.

2 Lightly grease and preheat a 4-hole (⅓-cup/80ml) pie maker.

3 Pour a scant ¼ cup mixture into prepared holes. Close lid; cook for 6 minutes or until a skewer inserted into centre of one cake comes out clean. Gently remove cakes; transfer to a wire rack to cool. Repeat in batches with remaining mixture to make 10 cakes in total.

4 Meanwhile, to make white chocolate glaze, place chocolate and butter in a small heatproof bowl over a small saucepan of simmering water (don't let the base of the bowl touch the water); stir until melted. Remove the bowl from the heat; sift over the icing sugar. Add milk; stir to form a glaze of a coating consistency.

5 Combine cream cheese and ¼ cup white chocolate glaze in a small bowl until smooth. Spoon into a piping bag fitted with a 1cm (½in) piping nozzle.

6 Remove 1 teaspoon of cake from centre of each cake. Pipe cream cheese mixture into hollows.

7 Combine both coconuts in a bowl. Dip cakes in white chocolate glaze; drain off excess. Toss in coconut. Place on wire racks covered with baking paper. Refrigerate for 10 minutes or until set.

8 Just before serving, dust cakes with strawberry powder.

BIRTHDAY CONFETTI LAYER CAKES

PREP + COOK TIME
1 HOUR (+ COOLING & FREEZING)

MAKES 4

490g (15½oz) vanilla cupcake mix

2 eggs

¾ cup (180ml) milk

60g (2oz) butter, softened

2 tablespoons rainbow sprinkles

1 cup (170g) unicorn confetti

VANILLA BUTTERCREAM

250g (8oz) butter, softened

250g (8oz) packet vanilla buttercream icing mix

1 tablespoon milk

1 Lightly grease and preheat a 4-hole (⅓-cup/80ml) pie maker. Cover two wire racks with baking paper.

2 Reserve frosting from packet for vanilla buttercream. Beat cake mix, eggs, milk and butter in a large bowl with an electric mixer on low speed, until combined. Increase speed to high; beat until smooth. Stir through rainbow sprinkles.

3 Spoon level ¼ cup cake mixture into prepared holes. Close lid; cook for 8 minutes or until a skewer inserted into the centre of one cake comes out clean. Remove cakes; tansfer to wire racks to cool. Repeat in batches with remaining cake mixture to make 12 cakes in total; re-grease pie holes as needed.

4 Meanwhile, to make vanilla buttercream, beat butter in a large bowl with electric mixer until light and fluffy. Gradually add reserved frosting and buttercream icing mix, then milk; beat for 5 minutes or until smooth and fluffy.

5 To assemble, trim tops of cakes slightly so they are level. Spread one cake with 2 teaspoons vanilla buttercream; repeat layering with a second cake, then finish with a third cake, trimmed-side down, to form a flat top. Repeat with remaining cakes and more buttercream to make 4 three-layered cakes in total. Using a palette knife, spread remaining buttercream generously around the side and top of layer cakes to form neat tall cylinder shapes with a swirled top. Freeze cakes for 30 minutes or until buttercream is firm.

6 Place unicorn confetti on a tray; gently roll cakes in confetti to coat. Turn upright to serve.

GIN & TONIC SYRUP CAKES

PREP + COOK TIME
45 MINUTES

MAKES 12

540g (1lb) packet vanilla cake mix (see cook's note)

3 eggs

¾ cup (180ml) milk

80g (2½oz) butter, melted

⅓ cup (25g) desiccated coconut

4 baby cucumbers (qukes) (100g)

icing sugar (confectioners' sugar), to dust

GIN & TONIC SYRUP

½ cup (110g) caster sugar (superfine sugar)

¼ cup (60ml) gin

¼ cup (60ml) tonic water

2 kaffir lime leaves, shredded finely

1 Reserve frosting sachet from box for another use. Beat cake mix, eggs, milk and butter in a large bowl with an electric mixer on low speed until ingredients are smooth and combined. Fold in the coconut. (Makes 4 cups.)

2 Lightly grease and preheat a 4-hole (⅓-cup/80ml) pie maker.

3 Spoon ¼ cup cake mixture into prepared holes. Close lid; cook for 7 minutes or until just firm to the touch. Gently remove cakes; transfer to a wire rack. Repeat in batches with remaining cake mixture to make 12 cakes in total.

4 To make gin and tonic syrup, place sugar, gin, tonic water and lime leaves in a small saucepan; stir over low heat, without boiling, until sugar dissolves. Bring to the boil; boil without stirring for 2 minutes. (Makes ⅔ cup.)

5 Place cakes on a tray lined with baking paper. Poke holes in the top of the cakes with a skewer. Pour hot syrup over hot cakes. Leave cakes to cool.

6 Cut 2 cucumbers into rounds; cut remaining cucumbers lengthways into ribbons. Serve syrup cakes topped with cucumber and dusted with icing sugar.

COOK'S NOTE

We used a cake mix that included a sachet of frosting, but it is not used in this recipe. For a vanilla cake mix only, buy a 425g (13½oz) packet or similar weight.

SOFT-CENTRED CHOC HAZELNUT PUDDINGS

PREP + COOK TIME
35 MINUTES

MAKES 6

100g (3oz) butter, chopped

100g (3oz) dark (semi-sweet) chocolate, chopped coarsely

½ cup (110g) firmly packed brown sugar

2 eggs, beaten lightly

1 teaspoon vanilla extract

½ cup (75g) plain four (all-purpose flour)

1 tablespoon cocoa powder, plus extra to dust

¼ cup (85g) Nutella, plus extra to serve

12 Ferrero Rocher chocolates (240g)

1 Lightly grease and preheat a 4-hole (⅓-cup/80ml) pie maker.

2 Stir butter and chocolate in a saucepan over low heat for 5 minutes or until melted and smooth. Remove from heat. Stir in sugar, then eggs and vanilla. Sift flour and cocoa over chocolate mixture; stir until combined. (Makes 1½ cups.)

3 Spoon 2 tablespoons of mixture into each prepared hole. Drop 2 teaspoons Nutella and 1 Ferrero Rocher in the centre of each, then cover with another 1 tablespoon of mixture. Close the lid; cook for 12 minutes or until risen and firm to touch. Gently remove puddings. Repeat with remaining mixture, Nutella and 2 more Ferrero Rochers to make 6 puddings in total.

4 Serve warm puddings topped with extra Nutella and a Ferrero Rocher, then dust with cocoa.

BANANA CINNAMON FRENCH TOAST

PREP + COOK TIME
30 MINUTES

MAKES 8

4 eggs

½ cup (125ml) banana-flavoured milk

1 teaspoon ground cinnamon

8 brioche bread slices (480g)

25g (¾oz) butter, melted

1 small banana (130g), sliced thinly

cooking oil spray

salted caramel ice-cream and maple syrup, to serve

1 Whisk the eggs, flavoured milk and cinnamon in a large bowl until combined.

2 Using a 7cm (2¾in) round cutter, cut out two rounds from each brioche slice.

3 Using some of the melted butter, lightly grease then preheat a 4-hole (⅓-cup/80ml) pie maker.

4 Soak eight brioche rounds in the egg mixture for 15 seconds on each side.

5 Place 1 soaked brioche round into a prepared hole; top with 2 banana slices, then with a second soaked brioche round and 1 slice of banana. Repeat for remaining three holes. Spray tops with oil. Close lid; cook for 7 minutes or until egg mixture is cooked through and golden. Remove french toast pies; transfer to a wire rack.

6 Repeat steps 5 and 6, with remaining butter, brioche rounds, egg mixture and banana slices.

7 Serve warm french toast pies with ice-cream and maple syrup.

COOK'S NOTE

If you prefer, you could use Nutella, Biscoff spread or jam instead of dulce de leche.

CARAMEL SNOW CAKES

PREP + COOK TIME
35 MINUTES

MAKES 10

490g (15½oz) packet vanilla cupcake mix

2 eggs

½ cup (125ml) milk

60g (2oz) butter, softened

½ cup (160g) dulce de leche

whipped cream and icing sugar (confectioners' sugar), to serve

1 Lightly grease and preheat a 4-hole (⅓-cup/80ml) pie maker.

2 Beat cupcake mix, eggs, milk and butter in a large bowl with an electric mixer on low speed, until combined. Increase speed to high; beat until smooth.

3 Pour ¼ cup cake mixture into prepared holes. Close lid; cook for 8 minutes or until a skewer inserted into the centre of one cake comes out clean. Gently remove cakes; transfer to a wire rack. Repeat in batches with remaining mixture to make 10 cakes in total. Cool.

4 Split cakes in half. Spread 2 teaspoons of dulce de leche on base layer of each cake then with whipped cream and top cake layer. Dust with icing sugar.

GINGER SCONES

PREP + COOK TIME
35 MINUTES

MAKES 8

1 cup (150g) self-raising flour

⅛ teaspoon fine salt

⅓ cup (80ml) pouring cream, plus extra for brushing

⅓ cup (80ml) ginger beer

⅓ cup (60g) finely chopped crystallised ginger

2 teaspoons raw sugar

butter and honey, to serve

1 Sift flour and salt into a large bowl; make a well in the centre. Pour in cream and ginger beer. Using a knife, 'cut' liquid through flour until mixture just forms a soft sticky dough.

2 Turn dough out onto a floured surface, top with crystallised ginger; gently knead until incorporated and smooth. Press dough out evenly until 2cm (¾in) thick. Cut into 5cm (2in) rounds with a floured cutter; place on a baking-paper-lined tray, then cover loosely with baking paper (to prevent drying out). Gently knead scraps of dough together; repeat pressing and cutting, to make 8 scones in total.

3 Lightly grease and preheat a 4-hole (⅓-cup/80ml) pie maker.

4 Place four dough rounds into prepared holes; brush tops with extra cream and sprinkle with half the sugar. Close lid; cook for 12 minutes or until browned and scones sound hollow when tapped firmly on top with your fingers. Gently remove scones; transfer to a wire rack. Repeat with remaining dough rounds, extra cream and remaining sugar.

5 Serve scones straightaway with butter and honey.

CHURROS & CHOCOLATE SAUCE

PREP + COOK TIME
35 MINUTES

MAKES 8

2 sheets frozen butter puff pastry, thawed

40g (1½oz) butter, melted

¼ cup (55g) firmly packed brown sugar

1 teaspoon ground cinnamon

CHOCOLATE SAUCE

½ cup (125ml) milk

½ cup (165g) Nutella

1 teaspoon cornflour (cornstarch)

1 Lightly grease and preheat a 4-hole (⅓-cup/80ml) pie maker.

2 Using a 6cm (2½in) cutter, cut 16 rounds from puff pastry. Brush eight rounds with melted butter then top with remaining eight rounds. Press gently to join together.

3 Place four pastry stacks into prepared holes. Close lid; cook for 7 minutes. Brush tops with a little more melted butter; turn over. Close lid; cook for a further 2 minutes or until risen and golden. Remove pastries; transfer to a wire rack. Repeat with remaining pastry stacks and more butter.

4 Meanwhile, to make chocolate sauce, heat milk in a small saucepan until just simmering (not boiling). Whisk in Nutella and cornflour; continue whisking until the sauce starts to thicken. Pour into a small serving bowl.

5 Combine sugar and cinnamon in another small bowl. Working with one at a time, brush pastries generously with more melted butter, then toss in the cinnamon sugar to coat.

6 Serve churros straightaway with warm chocolate sauce.

BLUEBERRY LIME CHEESECAKES

PREP + COOK TIME
35 MINUTES
(+ REFRIGERATION)

MAKES 8

7 Anzac biscuits (90g)

30g (1oz) butter, melted

½ cup (75g) fresh or frozen blueberries, plus extra to serve

250g (8oz) cream cheese, softened

½ cup (110g) caster sugar (superfine sugar)

½ teaspoon vanilla extract

2 eggs

icing sugar (confectioners' sugar), to serve

BLUEBERRY LIME SAUCE

½ cup (75g) fresh or frozen blueberries

¼ cup (55g) caster sugar (superfine sugar)

¼ teaspoon cornflour (cornstarch)

1½ tablespoons lime juice

1 Place biscuits in a zip-top bag; seal bag. Using a rolling pin, crush biscuits into crumbs. Add melted butter to bag; seal bag. Massage bag until well combined. With 24 paper cupcake cases, stack three together to create 8 triple-layered cases. Press 1 heaped tablespoon biscuit mixture in the base of each layered case. Place cases on a tray; refrigerate for 10 minutes to firm.

2 If using frozen blueberries, thaw on a plate lined with paper towel.

3 Preheat a 4-hole (⅓-cup/80ml) pie maker.

4 Beat cream cheese, caster sugar, vanilla and eggs in a small bowl with an electric mixer until smooth. Fill four paper cases with cream cheese mixture until slightly under the rim. Gently place in pie maker holes then top each with an eighth of the blueberries. Close lid; cook for 8 minutes or until just set in the centre. Gently remove cheesecakes; transfer to a wire rack. Repeat with remaining paper cases, cream cheese mixture and blueberries. Cool.

5 Meanwhile, to make blueberry lime sauce, place ingredients in a medium microwave-safe bowl; microwave on HIGH (100%) for 4 minutes. Crush berries with a fork. Cook in microwave for a further 1 minute or until thickened.

6 Serve cheesecakes cooled or chilled, topped with blueberry lime sauce and extra blueberries. Just before serving, dust with icing sugar.

SPICED APPLE MUFFINS

PREP + COOK TIME
30 MINUTES

MAKES 8

100g (3oz) butter, softened

¾ cup (165g) firmly packed brown sugar

½ teaspoon vanilla extract

2 eggs

2 medium apples (300g), peeled, cored, chopped coarsely

¾ cup (110g) plain flour (all-purpose flour)

½ teaspoon bicarbonate of soda (baking soda)

½ teaspoon baking powder

2 teaspoons ground cinnamon

1 teaspoon ground ginger

¼ teaspoon ground nutmeg

icing sugar (confectioners' sugar), and butter, to serve

1 Beat softened butter, brown sugar and vanilla in a medium bowl with an electric mixer until pale and fluffy. Beat in eggs, until just combined, then chopped apple. Sift flour, bicarb, baking powder and spices over mixture; stir with a large spoon until combined.

2 Lightly grease and preheat a 4-hole (⅓-cup/80ml) pie maker.

3 Spoon a slightly heaped ¼ cup mixture into prepared holes. Close lid; cook for 10 minutes or until a skewer inserted into the centre of one muffin comes out clean. Remove muffins; transfer to a wire rack. Repeat with remaining mixture to make eight muffins in total.

4 Dust muffins with icing sugar; serve with butter.

CHEESY CHORIZO & ONION MUFFINS

PREP + COOK TIME
35 MINUTES

MAKES 8

1 cured chorizo (130g), chopped finely

1 egg

80g (2½oz) butter, melted

¾ cup (180ml) buttermilk

2 tablespoons caramelised onion, plus extra to serve

2 cups (300g) self-raising flour

2 green onions (scallions), sliced thinly, plus extra to serve

½ cup (50g) coarsely grated mozzarella

⅓ cup (25g) finely grated parmesan

80g (2½oz) mozzarella, cut into cubes

1 Preheat a 4-hole (⅓-cup/80ml) pie maker.

2 Divide chorizo into holes; cook for 3 minutes, stirring. Close lid; cook for a further 7 minutes or until browned. Remove chorizo; reserve ¼ cup.

3 Whisk egg, melted butter, buttermilk and caramelised onion together in a jug. Sift flour into a large bowl; pour in egg mixture, stir gently to combine. Add sliced green onion, grated cheeses and remaining chorizo; stir gently to combine. Do not over mix; mixture should be lumpy.

4 Spoon a heaped ¼ cup of mixture into holes. Push a cube of mozzarella into the centre of each, then top with half the reserved chorizo.

5 Close lid; cook for 3 minutes. Lift lid; place a wooden spoon or other 2cm (¾in) object on the edge of the pie maker to keep the lid slightly ajar. Partially close lid; cook for a further 6 minutes or until tops are golden and spring back when touched. Gently remove muffins; transfer to a wire rack. Wipe holes clean with paper towel. Repeat with remaining mixture and chorizo to make eight in total.

6 Serve muffins topped with extra caramelised onion and green onion.

COOK'S NOTE

For a smaller pie maker, cook one dumpling in each hole. To make four large open dumplings, place a wrapper in hole over water; fill with 2 tbsp mixture. Close lid; cook for 8 minutes.

PRAWN DUMPLINGS

PREP + COOK TIME
35 MINUTES

MAKES 16

150g (4½oz) peeled uncooked prawns (shrimp), chopped finely

½ teaspoon sesame oil

1½ tablespoons sake

1 teaspoon finely grated ginger

1 clove garlic, crushed

2 kaffir lime leaves, chopped finely

2 green onions (scallions), chopped finely

1 egg white, beaten lightly

16 gow gee wrappers (150g)

2 tablespoons light soy sauce

1 small red chilli, seeded, chopped finely

coriander (cilantro) leaves, to serve

1 Combine prawns, sesame oil, 2 teaspoons of the sake, the ginger, garlic, kaffir lime, green onion and egg white in a medium bowl. (Makes ⅔ cup.)

2 Place 2 teaspoons prawn mixture in the centre of each gow gee wrapper; lightly brush half the edge with water, fold over into a half moon shape to enclose the filling. Pleat the edges of the dumpling in order for it to stand upright.

3 Lightly grease and preheat a 4-hole (¾-cup/180ml) pie maker.

4 Place 1 tablespoon cold water in each hole. Place two dumplings, slightly on their side leaning up against each other in each hole. Close lid; cook for 10 minutes. Transfer dumplings to a serving plate. Repeat with more water (take care of the steam as the pie maker is now hot) and remaining dumplings; close lid, cook for 5 minutes (this batch of dumplings will cook faster as the pie maker is hotter).

5 For dipping sauce, combine remaining sake with soy sauce and chilli in a small bowl.

6 Serve dumplings with dipping sauce and coriander.

CHICKEN & SAGE SAUSAGE ROLLS

PREP + COOK TIMES
1 HOUR 30 MINUTES

MAKES 16

500g (1lb) minced (ground) chicken

1 small onion (80g), grated coarsely

2 cloves garlic, crushed

1 egg, beaten lightly

⅓ cup (40g) sage and onion stuffing mix

3 teaspoons worcestershire sauce

2 tablespoons finely chopped sage

1 tablespoon finely grated lemon rind

¼ cup (35g) dried cranberries

2 sheets frozen puff pastry, thawed

1 egg yolk, extra

16 small sage leaves

cranberry sauce, to serve

1 Combine chicken mince, grated onion, garlic, egg, stuffing mix, worcestershire sauce, sage, lemon rind and cranberries in a large bowl. (Makes 2¼ cups.)

2 Cut each pastry sheet in half. Place equal amounts of chicken mixture lengthways down the centre of each pastry piece; roll up tightly, from long side, to enclose filling. Using a serrated knife, trim ends, then cut each roll into four pieces; place rolls seam-side down on trays.

3 Whisk extra egg yolk with 2 teaspoons cold water in a small bowl. Brush rolls with egg wash. Cover; refrigerate until needed.

4 Lightly grease and preheat a 4-hole (⅓-cup/80ml) pie maker.

5 Place four sausage rolls, seam-side up, into prepared holes. Close lid; cook for 8-10 minutes or until golden. Carefully turn rolls over, place a sage leaf on top, close lid; cook for a further 8-10 minutes or until cooked through. Remove rolls; transfer to a wire rack. Wipe holes with paper towel; re-grease as required. Repeat cooking in batches with remaining sausage rolls and sage leaves.

6 Serve sausage rolls warm with cranberry sauce.

COOK'S NOTE

Cooked sausage rolls can be frozen for up to 3 months. Reheat from frozen in the pie maker for 8 minutes each side.

SILVERBEET-WRAPPED RED CURRY SALMON

PREP + COOK TIME
20 MINUTES

MAKES 4

½ cup (150g) thai red curry paste

¼ cup (60ml) coconut milk

1 teaspoon brown sugar

½ teaspoon fish sauce

1 kaffir lime leaf, shredded (optional)

360g (11½oz) centre-cut piece salmon fillet, boneless, skinless, cut into 4 pieces

4 silverbeet leaves (260g), white stalk removed

2 x 250g (8oz) packets coconut rice

lime wedges and coriander (cilantro) leaves, to serve

1 Stir curry paste, coconut milk, sugar, fish sauce and lime leaf in small bowl to combine.

2 In an ungreased 4-hole (⅓-cup/80ml) pie maker turned off, place the centre part of a silverbeet leaf into one hole, pressing down. Place a piece of salmon snugly inside. Drizzle 2 tablespoons curry sauce over salmon then wrap like a present, tucking in loose pieces of silverbeet. Repeat with remaining silverbeet leaves, salmon and curry sauce.

3 Turn pie maker on. Gently lower lid without clipping shut; cook for 9 minutes for medium-rare salmon or a further 3 minutes for cooked through. Carefully lift salmon parcels out with a spoon.

4 Meanwhile, heat coconut rice according to packet directions.

5 Serve salmon parcels on coconut rice with lime wedges and coriander.

THYME & PARMESAN RISOTTO CAKES

PREP + COOK TIME
45 MINUTES

MAKES 12

2 x 250g (8oz) packets brown rice and red rice infused with garlic and chilli

2 eggs

1½ cups (105g) panko (japanese) breadcrumbs

40g (1½oz) butter

1 tablespoon extra virgin olive oil

1 medium onion (150g), chopped finely

70g (2½oz) button mushrooms, chopped finely

2 cloves garlic, crushed

2 teaspoons chopped thyme

¾ cup (60g) finely grated parmesan

½ teaspoon vegetable or chicken stock powder

1½ tablespoons cornflour (cornstarch)

60g (2oz) gorgonzola, cut into 1cm (½in) cubes

cooking oil spray

1 Heat rice according to packet directions; set aside. Whisk eggs in a shallow bowl. Place breadcrumbs in a second shallow bowl.

2 Heat butter and oil in a large frying pan. Add onion; cook, stirring, for 3 minutes or until softened. Add mushrooms, garlic and thyme; cook, stirring, for a further 3 minutes or until mushrooms are softened. Remove pan from heat.

3 Add hot rice to hot mushroom mixture in pan with parmesan, stock powder, cornflour, 1 tablespoon water, 2 tablespoons of the breadcrumbs and one-third of the beaten egg; season and combine well. Cool.

4 Generously grease then preheat a 4-hole (⅓-cup/80ml) pie maker.

5 Shape scant ⅓-cups of rice mixture into 12 balls. Push a cube of gorgonzola into the centre of each ball; using damp hands roll into smooth balls. Dip rice balls in the remaining beaten egg, allowing excess to drain off; cover with breadcrumbs to coat all over.

6 Spray four coated rice balls with oil; place into prepared holes, flatten slightly. Close lid; cook for 7 minutes. Gently turn the risotto cakes over with a spoon. Close lid; cook for a further 7 minutes or until browned and firm. Carefully remove risotto cakes with a spoon; keep warm. Repeat cooking in batches with remaining coated rice balls and spraying with oil.

DINNER & DESSERT FOR ONE

PREP + COOK TIME 25 MINUTES MAKES 4

1 sheet frozen shortcrust pastry, thawed

1 sheet frozen puff pastry, thawed

1 egg, beaten lightly

garden salad and honey, to serve

BEEF IN A BLANKET

1 tablespoon softened butter

1 small clove garlic, crushed

2 teaspoons coarsely chopped flat-leaf parsley

70g (2½oz) beef eye-fillet

POTATO & PEAS

1 teaspoon gravy powder

160g (5oz) potato, sliced very thinly

cooking oil spray

⅓ cup (40g) peas, thawed, mashed with fork

BREAD ROLL

⅓ cup (50g) self-raising flour

2 tablespoons milk

2 tablespoons whole-egg mayonnaise

APPLE GALETTE

1 teaspoon butter, melted

½ small pink lady apple (130g), cored, sliced thinly

1 teaspoon brown sugar

1 Lightly grease and preheat a 4-hole (⅓-cup/80ml) pie maker. Using pastry cutter provided, cut two large rounds (11cm/4½in) from shortcrust pastry and one small round (9.5cm/4in) from puff pastry.

2 To make beef in a blanket, combine butter, garlic and parsley in a small bowl. Line one prepared hole with a shortcrust pastry round, pressing into base and side. Place steak in pastry case, top with 2 teaspoons garlic butter (reserve remaining to serve). Top with puff pastry round; press edges firmly to seal. Brush pastry with egg.

3 To make potato & peas, combine gravy powder with 3 teaspoons boiling water. Layer slices of potato over base and side of a second hole to form a potato case. Spray with oil. Fill potato case with peas and gravy. Arrange remaining potato slices, slightly overlapping, to cover filling. Spray with oil.

4 To make bread roll, stir ingredients together in a small bowl to form a lumpy thick batter. Drop mixture into a third hole.

5 To make apple galette, place remaining shortcrust pastry round in the fourth hole, pressing into base and side; brush with a little of the melted butter. Arrange apple slices, slightly overlapping in pastry case. Brush with remaining melted butter, then sprinkle with sugar.

6 Close lid; cook beef in a blanket for 13 minutes for medium-rare. Cook potato & peas for 12 minutes or until potato is golden. Cook bread roll for 10 minutes or until doubled in sized and golden. Cook apple galette for 9 minutes or until pastry is golden. Once everything is cooked, turn off the pie maker and leave the apple galette in the machine to keep warm until ready to eat.

7 To serve, spread bread roll with remaining garlic butter. Place beef in a blanket on a serving plate with potato & peas, bread roll and garden salad. For dessert, serve warm apple galette, drizzled with a little honey.

VEGIE SAN CHOY BAU

PREP + COOK TIME
20 MINUTES

MAKES 8

- **1 teaspoon sesame oil, plus extra to brush**
- **⅔ cup (90g) quorn mince (meat free mince)**
- **225g (7oz) can water chestnuts, diced**
- **1 clove garlic, chopped finely**
- **1 teaspoon finely grated ginger**
- **3 green onions (scallions), white part sliced, green tops reserved**
- **1 tablespoon vegetarian oyster sauce**
- **½ teaspoon kecap manis**
- **1 teaspoon soy sauce**
- **8 wonton wrappers (55g)**
- **8 gem lettuce leaves**
- **2 tablespoons crushed roasted peanuts**
- **coriander (cilantro) leaves and sriracha, to serve**

1 Heat a small frying pan over medium heat; cook sesame oil, quorn mince, water chestnuts, garlic, ginger, white part of green onion, oyster sauce, kecap manis and soy, stirring, for 3 minutes or until heated through.

2 Brush four wonton wrappers on both sides with extra sesame oil and press into an ungreased 4-hole (⅓-cup/80ml) pie maker. Turn machine on. Close lid; cook for 5 minutes or until golden and crisp. Remove wonton cases; transfer to a wire rack. Repeat with remaining wonton wrappers and extra sesame oil.

3 Fill each wonton case with 2 heaped tablespoons quorn mixture, then place on a lettuce leaf. Serve san choy bau topped with peanuts, thinly sliced reserved green onion tops, coriander leaves and sriracha.

MI GORENG NOODLE PIES

PREP + COOK TIME
20 MINUTES

MAKES 4

85g (3oz) packet mi goreng flavoured instant noodles

⅔ cup (50g) shredded cabbage

½ small carrot (35g), cut into julienne

4 eggs (50g each)

1 tablespoon sriracha

fried shallots and garden salad, to serve

1 Prepare noodles following packet directions.

2 Generously oil and preheat a 4-hole (⅓-cup/80ml) pie maker.

3 Place equal amounts of cabbage and carrot into each hole and move around with chopsticks for 30 seconds until softened. Divide prepared noodles into holes, pressing down lightly. Crack an egg into each hole. Place a wooden spoon or other 2cm (¾in) object on the edge of the pie maker to keep the lid slightly ajar. Partially close lid; cook for 10-12 minutes for slightly gooey eggs, or until cooked to your liking. Carefully remove pies with a spoon.

4 To serve, drizzle hot pies with sriracha then sprinkle with fried shallots. Serve with garden salad.

MEDITERRANEAN VEGIE STACKS

PREP + COOK TIME
20 MINUTES

MAKES 4

1 small potato (120g)
100g (3oz) chargrilled eggplant
100g (3oz) chargrilled red capsicum (bell pepper)
100g (3oz) chargrilled zucchini strips
100g (3oz) haloumi
olive oil cooking spray

BASIL SAUCE
½ cup basil leaves
½ cup baby spinach leaves, plus extra to serve
1 tablespoon olive oil
1 clove garlic, crushed
2 tablespoons lemon juice
20g (¾oz) walnuts

1 Peel potato; using a mandoline, V-slicer or sharp knife, cut potato into thin rounds. Pat chargrilled eggplant, capsicum and zucchini dry with paper towel then cut into equal pieces. Cut haloumi into 5mm (¼in) slices.

2 Grease a 4-hole (⅓-cup/80ml) pie maker. Arrange three potato slices over base and side of each prepared hole. Turn pie maker on. Layer slices of eggplant, capsicum, zucchini and haloumi in each potato case. Top with more slices of potato to cover; spray with oil. Close lid; cook for 12 minutes or until potato is well browned and cooked.

3 Meanwhile, to make basil sauce, process or blend ingredients in a small food processor or blender with 2 tablespoons water until smooth. Season to taste.

4 Serve vegie stacks hot or at room temperature with basil sauce and extra spinach leaves.

COOK'S NOTE

For a smaller pie maker, trim muffin rounds, using a 6cm (2½in) cutter.

COOK'S NOTE

Turn unused burger bun bases into breadcrumbs; chop, then pulse in a food processor until coarse. Crumbs can be frozen for 1 month.

MUSHROOM CHEESE BURGER PIES

PREP + COOK TIME
20 MINUTES

MAKES 4

4 sheets frozen shortcrust pastry, thawed

4 sesame brioche burger buns (300g)

1 tablespoon butter, softened

4 thyme sprigs

4 white flat mushrooms (200g)

8 cheddar sandwich slices (160g)

½ cup (160g) caramelised onion relish

2 tablespoons dijon mustard

½ cup (105g) sliced bread and butter pickles, plus extra to serve

⅓ cup roasted red capsicum (bell pepper), chopped coarsely

sweet potato fries, to serve

1 Using pastry cutter provided for a 4-hole (¾-cup/180ml) pie maker, cut four large (15.5cm/6¼in) rounds from shortcrust pastry. Refrigerate until required.

2 Split burger buns in half; set bases aside for another use (see cook's note).

3 Preheat a 4-hole (¾-cup-180ml) pie maker.

4 Brush pie maker holes with the butter. Place a sprig of thyme in each prepared hole, followed by a mushroom, stalk facing down. Close lid; cook for 5 minutes or until softened. Remove mushrooms and thyme; drain on paper towel. Wipe holes clean with paper towel.

5 Line cleaned holes with pastry rounds; carefully press into base and sides. Prick pastry bases well with a fork. Close lid; cook for 3 minutes or until pastry is light golden.

6 Place one cheddar slice in each pastry case, then top with a mushroom, stalk-side up, onion relish, mustard, half the pickles, the capsicum, remaining pickles and remaining cheddar. Position bun tops to cover filling. Place a heatproof 3.5cm (1½in) object on the edges of the pie maker to keep the lid ajar. Partially close lid, taking care not to flatten the bun top. Cook for 8 minutes or until pastry is cooked and burger is heated through.

7 Serve burgers straightaway with hot sweet potato fries and extra sliced pickles.

DEEP-DISH MINI PIZZAS

PREP + COOK TIME
40 MINUTES

MAKES 8

2 x 250g (8oz) packets ready-made pizza dough

2 tablespoons pasta sauce

2 bocconcini (70g), sliced

2 tablespoons finely chopped truffle salami

2 tablespoons finely chopped drained roasted capsicum (bell pepper)

small basil leaves, to serve

1 Lightly grease and preheat a 4-hole (⅓-cup/80ml) pie maker.

2 Press dough balls together to form one. Roll out pizza dough ball on a lightly floured surface until 5mm (¼in) thick. Using a 9cm (3¾in) round cutter, cut 8 rounds from pizza dough. (Keep dough scraps for another use; see page 157.) Cover four dough rounds with baking paper to prevent dough from drying out.

3 Lift remaining four dough rounds into prepared holes; press lightly up the side. Close lid; cook for 5 minutes. Turn bases over; spread each round with 1 teaspoon pasta sauce, then top evenly with half each of the bocconcini, salami and capsicum. Close lid; cook for a further 7 minutes until cheese is lightly golden. Remove pizzas; transfer to a wire rack covered with baking paper. Repeat with remaining dough rounds and pasta sauce, then bocconcini, salami and capsicum.

4 To serve, top pizzas with small basil leaves.

COOK'S NOTE
For a non-vegetarian option, use chicken or pork mince instead. Cook the mince and listed ingredients in step 1 for 5 minutes.

COOK'S NOTE

Mi goreng is a dry-style Indonesian instant noodle available from supermarkets.

JAMMY BERRY PASTRIES

PREP + COOK TIME
40 MINUTES

MAKES 8

2 x 52g (1½oz) Cherry Ripe chocolate bars

80g (2½oz) Lindt Excellence Milk Chocolate

2 sheets frozen puff pastry, thawed

2 tablespoons raspberry jam

1 egg, beaten lightly

1 Lightly grease and preheat a 4-hole (⅓-cup/80ml) pie maker. Cut eight 5cm x 15cm (2in x 6in) strips of baking paper.

2 Cut each Cherry Ripe bar crossways into four pieces. Break milk chocolate into eight squares, following markings (you will have two squares leftover); cut each square in half to make 16 pieces.

3 Cut four 9cm (3¾in) squares from each pastry sheet. Place baking paper strips on a work surface; top with pastry squares in the centre. Place 1 teaspoon raspberry jam in the centre of each pastry square, then add 2 pieces of chocolate and 1 piece Cherry Ripe. Fold opposite corners of pastry toward the centre to partially cover the filling; brush pastry with egg.

4 Using baking paper strips, lift four pastries into prepared holes. Close lid; cook for 16 minutes or until golden brown. Use paper strips to remove pastries; transfer to a wire rack. Repeat with remaining pastries.

5 Serve pastries straightaway.

RICOTTA, PEA & MINT QUICHES

PREP + COOK TIME 40 MINUTES

MAKES 8

2 sheets frozen shortcrust pastry, thawed

3 eggs

100g (3oz) firm ricotta, crumbled

75g (2½oz) goat's cheese, crumbled

¼ cup finely chopped mint

1 cup (120g) frozen peas, thawed

2 green onions (scallions), chopped finely

2 teaspoons extra virgin olive oil

¼ cup small mint leaves, extra

1 Using pastry cutter provided for a 4-hole (⅓-cup/80ml) pie maker, cut eight large rounds (11cm/4½in) from shortcrust pastry. Refrigerate until required.

2 Whisk eggs, ricotta and 50g (1½oz) goat's cheese in a large jug. Stir in chopped mint. Season with salt and pepper.

3 Grease a 4-hole (⅓-cup/80ml) pie maker. With pie maker turned off, line prepared holes with pastry rounds; press into base and side.

4 Place 2 teaspoons peas and 1 teaspoon green onion into pastry cases. Spoon 1½ tablespoons egg mixture into each case.

5 Turn pie maker on. Close lid; cook for 10 minutes or until top is golden and egg is set. Gently remove quiches; transfer to a wire rack. Repeat with remaining pastry rounds, peas, green onion and egg mixture.

6 Lightly crush remaining peas and olive oil in a small bowl.

7 To serve, top quiches with goat's cheese, crushed pea mixture and extra mint leaves. Season with freshly ground black pepper.

COOK'S NOTE

For savoury crumpets, replace the vanilla bean paste with chilli flakes and a pinch of salt. Serve crumpets with poached eggs and avocado.

CRUMPETS

PREP + COOK TIME
35 MINUTES
(+ STANDING)

MAKES 8

½ cup (80g) wholemeal spelt flour
¼ cup (25g) rolled oats
¾ cup (180ml) milk
¾ teaspoon dried yeast
¼ teaspoon bicarbonate of soda (baking soda)
1 teaspoon vanilla bean paste
mascarpone, blueberry jam, honey and blueberries, to serve

1 Place flour, oats, milk, yeast, bicarb and vanilla in a medium bowl; whisk until combined. Cover; stand in a warm place for 1 hour or until bubbly and risen.

2 Lightly grease and preheat a 4-hole (⅓-cup/80ml) pie maker.

3 Pour 1 heaped tablespoon batter into prepared holes. Close lid; cook for 5 minutes or until starting to set and bubbles occur. Gently turn over with a small rubber spatula. Close lid; cook for a further 3 minutes or until lightly browned. Remove crumpets; transfer to a wire rack covered with baking paper. Repeat with remaining mixture.

4 To serve, top crumpets with mascarpone, jam, a drizzle of honey and blueberries.

SPAGHETTI VEGIE PIES

PREP + COOK TIME
35 MINUTES

MAKES 8

150g (4½oz) spaghetti

60g (2oz) butter

1 small leek (200g), white part only, sliced thinly

3 cloves garlic, crushed

1 cup (80g) broccoli florets, chopped finely

2 cups (70g) firmly packed baby spinach leaves

3 eggs, beaten lightly

1 cup (80g) coarsely grated parmesan

1 large zucchini (150g), spiralised

cooking oil spray

1 Break spaghetti in half; cook in a large saucepan of boiling salted water for 8 minutes or until al dente. Drain; return to pan. Cool slightly.

2 Heat butter in a large frying pan over medium heat; cook leek, garlic and broccoli, stirring, for 5 minutes or until softened. Add spinach; cook for a further 2 minutes or until wilted. Cool slightly.

3 Process broccoli mixture, egg, half the parmesan and ¼ cup water until smooth. (Makes 1¾ cups.)

4 Add blended vegetable mixture to spaghetti with spiralised zucchini; stir to coat spaghetti. (Makes 4 cups.)

5 Lightly grease and preheat a 4-hole (⅓-cup/80ml) pie maker.

6 Using a fork, twist approximately ½ cup spaghetti mixture around a fork. Push mixture from fork into prepared holes; spray with oil then sprinkle each with some of the remaining parmesan. Close lid; cook for 12 minutes or until firm and golden. Gently remove pies with a spoon; transfer to a wire rack covered with baking paper. Wipe holes clean with paper towel; lightly grease. Repeat with remaining spaghetti mixture and parmesan to make eight in total.

COOK'S NOTE

You can use 400g (12½oz) leftover cooked spaghetti, if you like. These little pies make perfect lunch box fillers for the kids.

MEDITERRANEAN QUICHES

PREP + COOK TIME
30 MINUTES

MAKES 8

4 eggs

½ cup (125ml) pouring cream

2 teaspoons finely chopped oregano, plus extra leaves to serve

2 sheets frozen puff pastry, thawed

32 baby spinach leaves

125g (4½oz) sundried tomatoes, drained

8 whole artichoke hearts in brine, drained, halved

16 pitted kalamata olives

50g (1½oz) mozzarella, cut into 1cm (¾in) cubes

pinch chilli flakes

1 Lightly grease and preheat a 4-hole (⅓-cup/80ml) pie maker.

2 Whisk eggs, cream and chopped organo together in a jug. Season.

3 Using pastry cutter provided, cut eight large rounds (11cm/4½in) from puff pastry. Line prepared holes with pastry rounds; pressing into base and side. Refrigerate remaining rounds until required.

4 Place 4 spinach leaves in each pastry case; top with a piece of sundried tomato, 2 artichoke halves and 2 olives. Pour 2 tablespoons of egg mixture over filling then top each with 1 cube of mozzarella and chilli flakes. Close lid; cook for 6 minutes or until filling is set. Remove quiches; transfer to a wire rack. Repeat with remaining pastry rounds, spinach leaves, sundried tomato, artichoke halves, olives, egg mixture, mozzarella and chilli flakes.

5 Serve quiches topped with extra oregano leaves.

CREPES SUZETTE

PREP + COOK TIME
50 MINUTES

MAKES 12

We used a family-size pie maker for this recipe.

350g (11oz) pancake mix

4 medium oranges (960g), peeled, white pith removed, cut into 5mm (¼in) rounds

ORANGE LIQUEUR SAUCE

125g (4oz) butter

¾ cup (165g) caster sugar (superfine sugar)

1½ cups (375ml) orange juice

⅓ cup (80ml) Cointreau (see cook's note)

1 Lightly grease and preheat a family-size (2½-cup/625ml) pie maker. Line the pie maker with a 12cm x 40cm (4¾in x 16in) piece of baking paper.

2 To make orange liqueur sauce, melt butter in a medium saucepan. Add sugar; cook over a low heat until sugar dissolves and begins to caramelise. Stir in orange juice and Cointreau; cook for 10 minutes or until sauce has reduced slightly. (Makes 1½ cups.)

3 Place pancake mix in a large bowl; gradually whisk in 2 cups (500ml) cold water until it forms a smooth batter. (Makes 3 cups.)

4 Pour ¼ cup batter into prepared hole. Close lid; cook for 1 minute or until crepe starts to set. Gently turn over with a rubber spatula. Close lid; cook for another 1 minute or until lightly browned. Remove crepe; transfer to a tray lined with baking paper. Repeat with remaining batter to make 12 crepes in total.

5 Fold crepes into quarters; serve topped with orange slices and orange liqueur sauce.

COOK'S NOTE

You can use your favourite orange liqueur instead of Cointreau, if you prefer. For an alcohol-free version, increase the orange juice to 2 cups (500ml).

MILLIONAIRE'S SHORTBREAD ROLLS

PREP + COOK TIME
35 MINUTES

MAKES 8

We used a 4-hole sausage roll maker for this recipe.

2 sheets frozen shortcrust pastry, thawed

⅔ cup (240g) Nutella, plus extra to serve (optional)

6 Arnotts Scotch Fingers (108g)

⅓ cup (110g) canned caramel top 'n' fill

1 egg yolk

1 Grease a 4-hole (2-tablespoon) sausage roll maker.

2 Cut each pastry sheet in half. With the sausage roll maker turned off, position a half pastry sheet to cover all holes; press pastry gently into each hole.

3 Spoon 1 tablespoon Nutella into each hole. Snap biscuits lengthways into fingers then snap four fingers in half. Place 1½ fingers on Nutella in a line then top each with 2 teaspoons caramel. Place a half sheet of pastry on top, press to seal pastry edges.

4 Whisk egg yolk and 1 tablespoon water in a small bowl. Brush pastry with egg wash.

5 Close lid; cook for 7 minutes. Carefully turn rolls over. Close lid; cook for a further 7 minutes or until golden. Remove rolls; transfer to a wire rack. Repeat with remaining pastry halves, Nutella, biscuit fingers, caramel and egg wash. Using a sharp knife, cut to separate rolls if necessary.

6 Serve rolls warm or cold with extra Nutella, if you like.

VARIATIONS

Outrageous rolls Swap Nutella for sweetened peanut butter and poke in as many mini M&M's as will fit. Continue as directed in the recipe.

Peppermint rolls Omit caramel. Finely chop 2 x 35g (1oz) Peppermint Crisp bars. Spoon Nutella into each hole; top with 1 shortbread finger and an eighth of the chopped Peppermint Crisp bar. Continue as directed in the recipe.

RASPBERRY COCONUT PIE

PREP + COOK TIME
25 MINUTES

SERVES 8

We used a family-size pie maker for this recipe.

1 cup (135g) fresh or frozen raspberries

1 egg

⅓ cup (80ml) pouring cream

½ teaspoon vanilla extract

1½ tablespoons caster sugar (superfine sugar)

1 tablespoon plain flour (all-purpose flour)

icing sugar (confectioners' sugar), to dust

COCONUT BASE

1 cup (75g) shredded coconut

½ cup (110g) caster sugar (superfine sugar)

¼ cup (35g) plain flour (all-purpose flour)

1 egg, beaten lightly

1 If using frozen raspberries, thaw on a plate lined with paper towel.

2 Using cutter provided with a family-size (2½-cup/625ml) pie maker, trace a 23cm (9¼in) round on baking paper; cut out round. Snip the edge of the paper round at four equal points so it will partially line the side of the pie hole.

3 To make coconut base, combine ingredients in a medium bowl.

4 In another medium bowl, whisk egg, cream, vanilla, caster sugar and flour until smooth and combined.

5 With the pie maker turned off, lightly grease a family-size (2½-cup/625ml) pie maker, then line with the paper round. Press coconut mixture over base and up the side, finishing just below the fluted rim. Turn pie maker on. Close lid without clipping shut; cook for 4 minutes (it will still be quite soft).

6 Lift lid; arrange raspberries over the base. Pour egg mixture over berries. Close lid; cook for a further 9 minutes or until just set in the centre. Carefully lift pie out by the paper sides; stand until cooled.

7 Serve pie dusted with icing sugar.

BLUEBERRY HAND PIES

PREP + COOK TIME
20 MINUTES

MAKES 4

We used a 4-hole sausage roll maker for this recipe.

30g (1oz) desiccated coconut

2 teaspoons cornflour (cornstarch)

2 tablespoons caster sugar (superfine sugar), plus extra to serve

1 teaspoon vanilla bean paste

10g (½oz) butter, chopped

1 sheet frozen puff pastry, thawed

80g (2½oz) fresh blueberries, plus extra to serve

1 egg yolk

1 Combine coconut, cornflour, sugar and vanilla in a small bowl. Rub in butter with your fingertips.

2 Grease a 4-hole (2-tablespoon) sausage roll maker.

3 Cut pastry sheet in half. With the sausage roll maker turned off, position a half pastry sheet to cover all holes; press pastry gently into each hole.

4 Divide coconut mixture equally into the holes, then top with berries. Place remaining half sheet of pastry on top; press to seal pastry edges.

5 Whisk egg yolk and 1 tablespoon water in a small bowl. Brush pies with egg wash.

6 Turn sausage roll maker on. Close lid; cook for 7 minutes. Carefully turn pies over. Close lid; cook for a further 7 minutes or until golden. Remove hand pies; transfer to a wire rack, then sprinkle with extra sugar. Using a sharp knife, cut to separate pies if necessary.

7 Serve hand pies straightaway with extra blueberries.

VARIATION

Raspberry & almond Swap coconut for ground almonds and blueberries for raspberries.

COOK'S NOTE

Cooked blueberry hand pies can be frozen for 3 months. Reheat from frozen in the sausage roll maker for 8 minutes each side.

COOK'S NOTE

Cooked spring rolls can be frozen for 2 months. Reheat from frozen in sausage roll maker for 8 minutes each side. Unused spring roll pastry sheets can be refrozen.

VEGIE & SRIRACHA SPRING ROLLS

PREP + COOK TIME
35 MINUTES

MAKES 12

We used a 4-hole sausage roll maker for this recipe.

2 x 50g (1½oz) packets vermicelli rice noodles

¼ cup (60ml) olive oil

350g (11oz) packet Superfood Veg Mix

1 clove garlic, crushed

2 teaspoons finely grated ginger

1 teaspoon sesame oil

2 tablespoons sriracha

1½ tablespoons oyster sauce

250g (8oz) packet frozen spring roll pastry sheets (21.5cm/8¾in square), thawed

soy sauce, to serve

1 Place rice noodles in a medium heatproof bowl; cover with boiling water. Stand for 2 minutes. Drain; rinse under cold water then return to the bowl. Using scissors, cut noodles into shorter lengths.

2 Heat 1 tablespoon of the olive oil in a large non-stick frying pan. Add 250g (8oz) veg mix, the garlic and ginger; cook, stirring, for 3 minutes or until vegies have softened.

3 Add vegie mixture to noodles with sesame oil, sriracha and oyster sauce; toss well to combine.

4 Preheat a 4-hole (2-tablespoon) sausage roll maker. Remove pastry from packet; keep covered with a tea towel to prevent drying out while working in batches.

5 Peel off one pastry sheet; place on a work surface. Brush with a little of the remaining olive oil, then turn sheet over. Place ⅓ cup of vegie filling 4cm (1½in) up from bottom edge, in a 10cm (4in) log shape. Fold bottom edge of pastry over filling, roll over once; fold in sides, then roll up to enclose filling. Repeat to make four spring rolls.

6 Place four spring rolls in holes. Close lid; cook for 8 minutes or until golden, turning over, if necessary halfway through cooking. Remove spring rolls; cover to keep warm.

7 Repeat steps 5 and 6, in batches, with eight more pastry sheets and remaining olive oil and vegie filling to make 12 spring rolls in total.

8 Serve spring rolls with soy sauce.

SILVERBEET & FETTA ROLLS

PREP + COOK TIME
35 MINUTES

MAKES 8

We used a 4-hole sausage roll maker for this recipe.

80g (2½oz) trimmed silverbeet
200g (6½oz) fetta, crumbled
2 tablespoons chopped dill
1 shallot, chopped finely
2 tablespoons extra virgin olive oil
2 sheets frozen shortcrust pastry, thawed
1 egg yolk
1½ tablespoons sesame seeds
spicy tomato relish, to serve

1 Finely chop silverbeet leaves; you will need 1½ cups firmly packed. Place silverbeet in a heatproof bowl; pour over boiling water. Drain immediately into a sieve and cool under cold running water. Squeeze out excess water; return to bowl.

2 Add fetta to spinach in bowl with dill, shallot and 1 teaspoon of the olive oil; toss well to combine. Season generously with ground black pepper. (Makes 2 cups.)

3 Grease a 4-hole (2-tablespoon) sausage roll maker.

4 Cut each pastry sheet in half. With the sausage roll maker turned off, position a half pastry sheet to cover all holes; press pastry gently into each hole. Fill each hole with ¼ cup spinach mixture. Place a half sheet of pastry on top, press to seal pastry edges.

5 Beat egg yolk and 1 teaspoon cold water in a small bowl. Brush rolls with egg wash; sprinkle each with ½ teaspoon sesame seeds.

6 Turn sausage roll maker on. Close lid; cook for 7 minutes. Carefully turn rolls over. Close lid; cook for a further 7 minutes or until golden. Remove rolls; transfer to a wire rack. Repeat with remaining pastry halves, spinach mixture, egg wash and sesame seeds. Using a sharp knife, cut to separate rolls if necessary.

7 Serve rolls with tomato relish.

COOK'S NOTE

Cooked spinach and fetta rolls can be frozen for 2 months. Reheat from frozen in sausage roll maker for 8 minutes each side.

ANY SAUSAGE ROLL

PREP + COOK TIME
35 MINUTES

MAKES 6

We used a 4-hole sausage roll maker for this recipe.

1 egg yolk

6 sausages (500g) (see build your own)

2 tablespoons caramelised onion relish

1½ sheets frozen puff pastry, thawed

1 Grease a 4-hole (2-tablespoon) sausage roll maker. Whisk egg yolk with 1 tablespoon water in a small bowl.

2 Cut a slit at the top of each sausage and squeeze out sausage meat from casings into a bowl. Add onion relish; stir to combine.

3 Cut whole pastry sheet in half. With the sausage roll maker turned off, position a half pastry sheet to cover all holes; press pastry gently into each hole. Fill each hole with a sixth of the sausage mixture. Place a half sheet of pastry on top, press to seal pastry edges. Brush with egg wash. Using a small sharp knife, cut three slashes along the top of each sausage roll.

4 Turn sausage roll maker on. Close lid; cook for 6 minutes. Turn sausage rolls over. Close lid; cook for a further 6 minutes or until golden. Transfer to a wire rack.

5 Cut remaining half pastry sheet crossways in half. Position one piece of pastry to cover the left front and back two holes. Press pastry gently into holes. Fill each hole with remaining sausage mixture. Place remaining piece of pastry on top; press to seal pastry edges. Using a sharp knife, cut to separate rolls if necessary.

6 Serve rolls straightaway with suggested condiment.

BUILD YOUR OWN

Lamb, rosemary & fetta sausages
+ 2 tbsp caramelised onion relish.
Serve with mint sauce.

Italian pork sausages
+ 1 tbsp caramelised onion relish
+ 1 tbsp apple sauce.
Serve with extra apple sauce.

Beef & garlic sausages
+ 1 tbsp tomato sauce (ketchup)
+ 1 tbsp chopped sweet pickles.
Serve with extra tomato sauce.

Plant-based sausages
+ 2 tbsp beetroot relish.
Serve with tzatziki.

SCRAP HACKS

Don't throw it save it! Store your pastry or dough scraps and off-cuts flat in the freezer to use at a later date. You can use any type of pastry or a combination to make these soup toppers, lunch box fillers or tasty snacks. Bake puff pastry at 200°C/400°F and shortcrust (or a mix of types) at 180°C/350°F. Cool and store in containers.

1 CHEESE STRAWS Roll pastry scraps out on a sheet of baking paper; brush with melted butter and sprinkle with finely grated parmesan. Cut into strips. Chill pastry in the freezer for 5 minutes. Separate the strips; roll in thin straws using both hands. Bake for 15 minutes or until golden.

2 SEEDED SOUP TOPPERS Gather pastry scraps, roll thinly; scatter with a single seed or combination of seeds (poppy seed, fennel, caraway or cumin are great options). Cut out using a small round cutter. Bake for 10 minutes.

3 THUMBPRINTS Gather pastry scraps, roll out thinly and stamp out using a small round cutter. Dollop a teaspoon of jam, curd or Nutella in the centre. Bake for 12 minutes.

4 FRECKLES Gather pastry scraps, roll out thinly and stamp out using a small round cutter. Scatter with 100's & 1,000's. Bake for 12 minutes.

5 NICE 'N' SPICY Gather pastry scraps, roll out thinly. Brush with a little sriracha; sprinkle with sesame seeds. Stamp out with your favourite cutter. Bake for 12 minutes.

6 OATIES Weigh pastry scraps; combine with an equal weight of rolled oats and ½ weight soft-salted butter. Roll out thinly; cut into diamonds. Bake for 10 minutes.

7 ORANGE POPPY SEED Gather pastry scraps, roll out thinly. Scatter with a combination of poppy seeds, finely grated orange rind and caster sugar; press down on pastry. Stamp out with a flower cutter or your favourite cutter. Bake for 12 minutes.

8 CINNAMON SPIRALS PIE CRUST Gather 200g (6½oz) pastry scraps; roll out to a 20cm x 30cm (8in x 12in) rectangle. Sprinkle with ¼ cup white sugar and 3 tsp ground cinnamon. Roll-up from a short end; cut into 2.5cm (1in) slices. Bake slices cut-side down for 10 minutes.

GLOSSARY

ALMONDS
flaked paper-thin slices.
meal also known as ground almonds.
BAKING PAPER also called parchment or baking parchment; a silicone-coated paper that is primarily used for lining baking pans and oven trays so cooked food doesn't stick, making removal easy.
BAKING POWDER a raising agent consisting mainly of two parts cream of tartar to one part bicarbonate of soda (baking soda).
BEEF
eye-fillet tenderloin, fillet; fine texture, most expensive and extremely tender.
minced also known as ground beef.
BREADCRUMBS
fresh are best made from bread that is slightly stale, about 3 days old. For fresh bread, leave the slices out on the bench for a few hours to dry out. Process bread, with, or without crusts, until coarse crumbs are formed.
panko (japanese) are available in two kinds: larger pieces and fine crumbs; have a lighter texture than Western-style ones. Available from Asian food stores and most supermarkets.
BUTTERMILK originally the term given to the slightly sour liquid left after butter was churned from cream, today it is made from no-fat or low-fat milk to which specific bacterial cultures have been added.
CAPSICUM (BELL PEPPER) comes in many colours: red, green, yellow and orange. Discard seeds and membranes before use.
CHEESE
brie soft-ripened cow-milk cheese with a delicate, creamy texture and a rich, sweet taste that varies from buttery to mushroomy. Best served at room temperature after a brief period of ageing, brie should have a bloomy white rind and creamy, voluptuous centre which becomes runny with ripening.
cheddar the most common cow's milk 'tasty' cheese; should be aged, hard and have a pronounced bite.
cream commonly called philadelphia or philly; a soft cow-milk cheese, its fat content ranges from 14 to 33%.
fetta a crumbly textured goat's- or sheep-milk cheese with a sharp, salty taste. Ripened and stored in salted whey.
goat's made from goat's milk, has an earthy, strong taste; available in soft and firm textures, in various shapes and sizes, and sometimes rolled in ash or herbs.
haloumi a Greek Cypriot cheese with a semi-firm, spongy texture and very salty sweet flavour. Ripened and stored in salted whey; best grilled or fried, and holds its shape well on being heated. Eat while still warm as it becomes tough and rubbery on cooling.
mozzarella soft, spun-curd cheese originating in southern Italy where it was traditionally made from water-buffalo milk. Now generally made from cow's milk, it is the most popular pizza cheese because of its low melting point and elasticity when heated.
parmesan also called parmigiano; is a hard, grainy cow-milk cheese originating in Italy. Reggiano is the best variety.
ricotta a soft, sweet, moist, white cow-milk cheese with a low fat content and a slightly grainy texture. The name roughly translates as 'cooked again' and refers to ricotta's manufacture from a whey that is itself a by-product of other cheese making.
CHICKEN
breast fillet breast halved, skinned and boned.
thigh skin and bone intact.
thigh cutlet thigh with skin and centre bone intact; sometimes found skinned with bone intact.
thigh fillet thigh with skin and centre bone removed.
CHILLI available in many types and sizes. Use rubber gloves when seeding and chopping fresh chillies as they can burn your skin. Removing membranes and seeds lessens the heat level.
flakes also sold as crushed chilli; dehydrated deep-red extremely fine slices and whole seeds.
green any unripened chilli; also some particular varieties that are ripe when green, such as jalapeño, habanero, poblano or serrano.
jalapeño pronounced hah-lah-pain-yo. Fairly hot, medium-sized, plump, dark green chilli; available pickled, canned or bottled, and fresh from greengrocers.
small red also known as thai or serrano; tiny, very hot and bright red in colour.
CHOCOLATE
dark (semi-sweet) also called luxury chocolate; made of a high percentage of cocoa liquor and cocoa butter, and little added sugar.
milk most popular eating chocolate, mild and very sweet; similar in make-up to dark chocolate with the difference being the addition of milk solids.
white contains no cocoa solids but derives its sweet flavour from cocoa butter. It is very sensitive to heat.
CHORIZO sausage of Spanish origin, made of coarsely ground pork and highly seasoned with garlic and chilli.

CINNAMON available in pieces (sticks or quills) and ground into powder; one of the world's most common spices, used as a sweet, fragrant flavouring for both sweet and savoury foods.

COCOA POWDER also known as unsweetened cocoa; cocoa beans (cacao seeds) that have been fermented, roasted, shelled, ground into powder then cleared of most of the fat content.

COCONUT

cream obtained commercially from the first pressing of the coconut flesh alone, without the addition of water; the second pressing (less rich) is sold as coconut milk. Available in cans and cartons at most supermarkets.

desiccated concentrated, dried, unsweetened and finely shredded coconut flesh.

flaked dried flaked coconut flesh.

milk not the liquid inside (coconut water), but the diluted liquid from the second pressing of the white flesh of a mature coconut.

shredded thin strips of dried coconut.

CORNFLOUR (CORNSTARCH) available from corn (100% maize) or wheat (wheaten cornflour, gives a lighter texture in cakes); used as a thickening agent.

CRANBERRIES available dried and frozen; has a rich, astringent flavour and can be used in sweet and savoury dishes. The dried version can usually be substituted for or with other dried fruit.

CREAM

pouring also called pure or fresh cream; it contains no additives and a minimum fat content of 35%.

thick (double) a dolloping cream with a minimum fat content of 45%.

thickened (heavy) a whipping cream that contains a thickener. It has a minimum fat content of 35%.

CRÈME FRAÎCHE a mature, naturally fermented cream with a velvety texture and slightly tangy, nutty flavour. Minimum fat content 35%. A French variation of sour cream, it boils without curdling and is used in sweet and savoury dishes.

CUMIN also called zeera or comino; resembling caraway in size, cumin is the dried seed of a plant related to the parsley family. Available dried as seeds or ground, it has a spicy, almost curry-like flavour.

CURRY PASTES commercially prepared curry pastes vary in strength and flavour; use whichever one you feel best suits your spice-level tolerance.

EDAMAME (SOYBEANS) are fresh soy beans in the pod; available frozen from Asian food stores and major supermarkets.

EGGPLANT also called aubergine. Ranging in size from tiny to very large and in colour from pale green to deep purple. Can also be purchased char-grilled, packed in oil, in jars.

EGGWASH beaten egg (white, yolk or both) and milk or water; often brushed over pastry or bread to impart colour or gloss.

FISH SAUCE also called nam pla or nuoc nam; made from pulverised salted fermented fish, most often anchovies. Has a pungent smell and strong taste, so use sparingly.

FLOUR

plain (all-purpose) unbleached wheat flour; is the best for baking as the gluten content ensures a strong dough for a light result.

self-raising all-purpose plain or wholemeal flour with baking powder and salt added; make at home in the proportion of 1 cup flour to 2 teaspoons baking powder.

wholemeal also called wholewheat flour; milled with the wheat germ so is higher in fibre and more nutritional than plain flour.

FOOD COLOURING vegetable-based substance available in liquid, paste or gel form.

GARAM MASALA a blend of spices that includes cardamom, cinnamon, coriander, cloves, fennel and cumin. Black pepper and chilli can be added for heat.

GINGER

fresh also called green or root ginger; thick gnarled root of a tropical plant.

ground also called powdered ginger; used as a flavouring in baking but cannot be substituted for fresh ginger.

KAFFIR LIME LEAVES also called bai magrood. Aromatic leaves of a citrus tree; two glossy dark green leaves joined end to end, forming a rounded hourglass shape. A strip of fresh lime peel may be substituted for each kaffir lime leaf.

KECAP MANIS a thick soy sauce with added sugar and spices. The sweetness comes from the addition of molasses or palm sugar.

MAPLE SYRUP distilled from the sap of sugar maple trees. Maple-flavoured syrup or pancake syrup is not an adequate substitute for the real thing.

MILK we use full-cream homogenised milk unless stated otherwise.

caramel top 'n' fill a canned milk product consisting of condensed milk that has been boiled to a caramel.

sweetened condensed a canned milk product consisting of milk with more than half the water content removed and sugar added to the remaining milk.

MISO fermented soybean paste. There are many types, each with its own aroma, flavour, colour and texture. It can be refrigerated in an airtight container for up to a year. Generally, the darker the miso, the saltier the taste and denser the texture.
MUSTARD, DIJON pale brown, distinctively flavoured, mild french mustard.
NUTMEG a strong and pungent spice ground from the dried nut of an evergreen tree native to Indonesia. Usually found ground, the flavour is more intense from a whole nut, available from spice shops, so it's best to grate your own.
OIL
cooking spray we use a cholesterol-free cooking spray made from canola oil.
olive made from ripened olives. Extra virgin and virgin are the first and second press, respectively, of the olives and are therefore considered the best; the 'extra light' or 'light' name on other types refers to taste not fat levels.
sesame used as a flavouring rather than for cooking.
vegetable oils sourced from plant fats.
ONIONS
green (scallions) also called, incorrectly, shallot; an immature onion picked before the bulb has formed, has a long, bright-green stalk.
shallots also called french or golden shallots or eschalots; small and brown-skinned.
spring an onion with a small white bulb and long, narrow green-leafed tops.
PAPRIKA ground dried sweet red capsicum (bell pepper); there are many grades and types available, including sweet, hot, mild and smoked.
PASTRY SHEETS ready-rolled packaged sheets of frozen puff and shortcrust pastry, available from supermarkets.
RHUBARB a plant with long, green-red stalks; becomes sweet and edible when cooked.
ROASTING/TOASTING desiccated coconut, pine nuts and sesame seeds roast more evenly if stirred over low heat in a heavy-based frying pan; their natural oils will help turn them golden. Remove from pan immediately. Nuts and dried coconut can be roasted in the oven to release their aromatic essential oils. Spread evenly onto an oven tray, roast at 180°C/350°F for about 5 minutes.
SILVERBEET (SWISS CARD) also called, incorrectly, spinach; has fleshy stalks and large leaves. Prepare as you would spinach.
SOUR CREAM thick, commercially cultured sour cream with a minimum fat content of 35%.
SPINACH also called english spinach and incorrectly, silver beet. Baby spinach leaves are eaten raw in salads or cooked until wilted.
SOY SAUCE made from fermented soya beans. Several varieties are available in supermarkets and Asian food stores. We use japanese soy sauce unless stated otherwise.
SUGAR
brown very soft, finely granulated sugar retaining molasses for its characteristic colour and flavour.
caster (superfine) finely granulated table sugar.
icing (confectioners') also called powdered sugar; pulverised granulated sugar crushed with a little cornflour (cornstarch).
pure icing (confectioners') powdered sugar.
raw natural brown granulated sugar.
SUMAC a purple-red, astringent spice ground from berries that grow around the Mediterranean; adds a tart, lemony flavour to dips and dressings and goes well with barbecued meat.
TOMATOES
canned whole peeled tomatoes in natural juices; available crushed, chopped or diced. Use undrained.
paste triple-concentrated tomato puree used to flavour soups, stews and sauces.
puree canned pureed tomatoes (not tomato paste); substitute with fresh peeled and pureed tomatoes.
VANILLA
bean paste made from vanilla pods and contains real seeds. Is highly concentrated; 1 teaspoon replaces a whole vanilla pod. Available in most supermarkets in the baking section.
extract made by extracting the flavour from the vanilla bean pod; pods are soaked, usually in alcohol, to capture the authentic flavour.
WORCESTERSHIRE SAUCE thin, dark-brown spicy sauce developed by the British when in India; used as a seasoning for meat, gravies and cocktails, and as a condiment.
YEAST (dried and fresh), a raising agent used in dough making. Granular (7g sachets) and fresh compressed (20g blocks) yeast can often be substituted for the other.
YOGHURT we use plain full-cream yoghurt unless noted otherwise.
ZUCCHINI also called courgette; small, pale- or dark-green or yellow vegetable of the squash family.

CONVERSION CHART

MEASURES

One Australian metric measuring cup holds approximately 250ml; one Australian metric tablespoon holds 20ml; one Australian metric teaspoon holds 5ml. The difference between one country's measuring cups and another's is within a two- or three-teaspoon variance and will not affect your cooking results. North America, New Zealand and the United Kingdom use a 15ml tablespoon. All cup and spoon measurements are level.

The most accurate way of measuring dry ingredients is to weigh them.

When measuring liquids, use a clear glass or plastic jug with the metric markings.

We use extra-large eggs with an average weight of 60g unless noted otherwise.

DRY MEASURES

metric	imperial
15g	½oz
30g	1oz
60g	2oz
90g	3oz
125g	4oz (¼lb)
155g	5oz
185g	6oz
220g	7oz
250g	8oz (½lb)
280g	9oz
315g	10oz
345g	11oz
375g	12oz (¾lb)
410g	13oz
440g	14oz
470g	15oz
500g	16oz (1lb)
750g	24oz (1½lb)
1kg	32oz (2lb)

OVEN TEMPERATURES

These oven temperatures are for conventional ovens; if you use a fan-forced ovens, decrease the temperature by 10-20 degrees.

	°C (Celsius)	°F (Fahrenheit)
Very slow	120	250
Slow	150	300
Moderately slow	160	325
Moderate	180	350
Moderately hot	200	400
Hot	220	425
Very hot	240	475

LIQUID MEASURES

metric	imperial
30ml	1 fluid oz
60ml	2 fluid oz
100ml	3 fluid oz
125ml	4 fluid oz
150ml	5 fluid oz
190ml	6 fluid oz
250ml	8 fluid oz
300ml	10 fluid oz
500ml	16 fluid oz
600ml	20 fluid oz
1000ml (1 litre)	1¾ pints

LENGTH MEASURES

metric	imperial
3mm	⅛in
6mm	¼in
1cm	½in
2cm	¾in
2.5cm	1in
5cm	2in
6cm	2½in
8cm	3in
10cm	4in
13cm	5in
15cm	6in
18cm	7in
20cm	8in
22cm	9in
25cm	10in
28cm	11in
30cm	12in (1ft)

INDEX

L

M

N

O

P

Q

R

S

T

V

Published in 2021 by Are Media Books, Australia.
Are Media Books is a division of Are Media Pty Limited.

ARE MEDIA

Chief executive officer
Brendon Hill

ARE MEDIA BOOKS

General manager: Publishing
Sally Eagle

Editorial & food director
Sophia Young

Creative director & designer
Hannah Blackmore

Managing editor Stephanie Kistner

Food editor Sophia Young

Operations manager David Scotto

Business development manager
Simone Aquilina
simone.aquilina@aremedia.com.au
Ph +61 2 8268 6278

Photographer Con Poulos

Stylists Olivia Blackmore, Lucy Tweed

Photochef Vikki Moursellas

Recipe developers Rebecca Lyall, Vikki Moursellas, Olivia Blackmore, Sophia Young, Sarah Murphy

Special thanks to Emma Knowles for her contribution of recipe ideas for this book.

Printed in China
by 1010 Printing International

A catalogue record for this book is available from the National Library of Australia.
ISBN 978-1-92586-585-1

Published by Are Media Books, a division of Are Media Pty Limited, 54 Park St, Sydney; GPO Box 4088, Sydney, NSW 2001, Australia
Ph +61 2 9282 8000;
www.awwcookbooks.com.au

International rights manager
Simone Aquilina
simone.aquilina@aremedia.com.au
Ph +61 2 8268 6278

Order books
phone 1300 322 007 (within Australia)

or order online at
www.awwcookbooks.com.au

Send recipe enquiries to
recipeenquiries@aremedia.com.au

 womensweeklyfood  @womensweeklyfood

PLOUGHMAN'S TOASTIE

PREP + COOK TIME
45 MINUTES

MAKES 4

4 english muffins (270g)

½ cup (145g) branston pickle

135g (4oz) sliced shaved leg ham

140g (4½oz) cheddar, cut into slices

cooking oil spray

boiled eggs and pickles, to serve

1 Lightly grease and preheat a 4-hole (¾-cup/180ml) pie maker.

2 Split muffins in half; line prepared holes with muffin bases. Top each with 1½ tablespoons branston pickle then equally divide with ham and cheddar slices. Position muffin tops over filling, then spray with oil.

3 Close lid; cook for 10 minutes or until bread is toasted and cheese has melted.

4 Serve toasties with boiled eggs and pickles.

SCOTCH EGGS

PREP + COOK TIME
40 MINUTES

MAKES 6

8 eggs, at room temperature

1 cup (75g) panko (japanese) breadcrumbs

⅓ cup (50g) plain flour (all-purpose flour)

500g (1lb) pork sausages

cooking oil spray

sriracha and baby kale leaves, to serve

1 Bring a large saucepan of water to the boil. Add 6 of the eggs; boil for 6 minutes. Transfer eggs to a bowl of iced water. When cool enough to handle, peel eggs.

2 Meanwhile, whisk remaining eggs in a shallow bowl. Place breadcrumbs and flour in two more shallow bowls.

3 Slit sausages at the top with a sharp knife; squeeze out sausage meat from casings. Divide sausage meat into six equal portions. Shape one portion evenly around each peeled egg. Coat scotch eggs in flour, shaking off excess. Dip in beaten egg, allowing excess to drain off, then cover gently in crumbs to coat all over.

4 Lightly grease and preheat a 4-hole (⅓-cup/80ml) pie maker.

5 Place four scotch eggs into prepared holes; spray tops with oil. Close lid; cook for 10 minutes for soft-centred eggs, or 13 minutes for well done eggs. Remove gently with a spoon; transfer to a wire rack covered with baking paper. Repeat with remaining scotch eggs.

6 Serve scotch eggs straightaway with sriracha and kale leaves.